Classic Crochet

The Modern Way

TOVE FEVANG

*Over 35 Fresh Designs Using
Traditional Techniques:
Placemats, Potholders, Bags,
Scarves, Mitts and More*

TRAFALGAR SQUARE
North Pomfret, Vermont

First published in the United States of America
in 2015 by
Trafalgar Square Books
North Pomfret, Vermont 05053

Originally published in Norwegian as *Klassisk hekling og hakking*.

ISBN: 978-1-57076-724-1

Library of Congress Control Number: 2015930001

Translator: Carol Huebscher Rhoades
Detail photography: Geir Arnesen
Other photography: Guri Pfeifer
Interior design: Lise Mosveen

Printed in China

10 9 8 7 6 5 4 3 2 1

Contents

Foreword

Crochet and Tunisian crochet are more popular than ever. Both are old techniques that are easy to learn if you haven't already. You just need a regular or Tunisian crochet hook and a ball of yarn to be on your way. These days a wide range of beautiful wool, alpaca, cotton, linen, silk, and cashmere yarns are available in all possible colors and weights.

I started crocheting when I was 5 or 6 years old and since then a crochet hook has never been far from my hands. I learned Tunisian crochet while studying textiles. Handcrafts are both my work and one of my leisure activities. Many of the items were made as I traveled here and there around the world. One particularly nice aspect of crochet is that it is easy to take along anywhere. It's relaxing to crochet at airports and on long flights. After a long day at the office, I can throw myself down on the sofa and be re-energized once I retrieve my crochet hook and yarn from the project basket.

The goal of this book is provide inspiration for whatever you want to create. If you haven't crocheted before, the last section of the book offers a "crochet school" so you can learn all the basic stitches and various crochet structures. What is exciting about regular and Tunisian crochet is that there are so many kinds of structures that can be combined. Nothing is absolutely right or crazy—combine, change colors or yarn and techniques, and make it your way. I most enjoy the process of a project, which is, for me, almost more important than the finished item. I also like having something in my hands to pass time and I am happy when the result is what I had envisioned.

If you have a crochet hook and some yarn, you have all you need to get started.

Good Luck!

Best wishes,
Tove
www.tovefevang.no

Washcloth

MEASUREMENTS:

Approx. 9½ x 9½ in / 24 x 24 cm

MATERIALS:

Yarn: CYCA #1, PT Pandora (100% pima cotton, 180 yd/165 m / 50 g)
Light Purple 237, 50 g
Beige 238, 50 g

Tunisian Crochet Hook: U.S. size I-9 / 5.5 mm
Crochet Hook: U.S. size F-5 / 3.75 mm for foundation chain and edging

GAUGE:

24 sts in Tunisian crochet pattern with larger hook = 4 in / 10 cm.
Adjust hook size to obtain correct gauge if necessary.

1 pattern repeat = 2 sts

Tunisian Crochet Stitches Used: Vertical stitch and twisted vertical stitch (see pages 122-123).
Crochet Stitches Used: Chain st (ch) and slip st (sl st) (see page 110).

Change colors on the return row, on the last step of the stitch just before the first new color stitch in Tunisian crochet. See page 124 for step-by-step instructions for changing colors. Using this method produces a "whole color" on the 1st st of the forward row.

Carry the color not in use for a row up the side.

INSTRUCTIONS:

With smaller size crochet hook and Beige, ch 62 sts.

Row 1, forward: Change to Tunisian crochet hook and begin in the 2nd ch from hook. Pick up 61 vertical sts in the top loop of each chain = 62 loops on the hook.

Row 1, return: Bind off each stitch as follows: Yarn around hook and through the first loop on the hook, *yarn around hook and through 2 loops on hook*; rep * to * across.

Row 2, forward: 1 edge st, pick up *1 vertical loop, 1 twisted vertical loop*; rep from * to * across, ending with 1 edge st = 62 sts on hook.

Row 2, return: Bind off all sts.

Row 3, forward and return: Work as for Row 2, forward and return. Change to Light Purple.

Rows 4-47, forward and return: Repeat Row 2, forward and return, working in stripe sequence as follows:

While working in pattern as for Row 2, forward and return throughout, repeat stripe sequence: *2 complete forward and return rows with Beige and 1 forward and return row with Light Purple*; rep * to * until there are 15 total repeats of the stripe pattern; end with 2 repeats of Beige. Change to Light Purple and smaller hook; finish with chain and slip sts as follows:

Insert crochet hook through *2 sts at the same time and join with 1 slip st, ch 1*; rep from * to * across, ending with 1 sl st into the edge st. Do not cut yarn, but, instead, continue around with the edging, beginning on the 1st long side.

Edging: With smaller hook, work 1 sl st in corner, work 1 sl st in each st along edge, 1 sl st in corner and then continue along the foundation chain with 1 sl st in each ch; 1 sl st in corner and then 1 sl st in each st along last long side; end with 1 sl st in the 1st sl st; cut yarn.

FINISHING:

Weave in all ends neatly. Lightly steam press the washcloth on the wrong side to finished measurements.

7

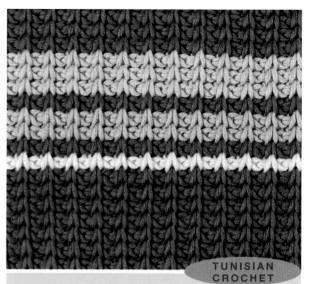

MEASUREMENTS:
Approx. 12¾ x 17¼ in / 32 x 44 cm

MATERIALS:
Yarn: CYCA #2, PT Petunia
(100% pima cotton, 120 yd/110 m / 50 g)
Gray-Purple 250, 100 g
Light Purple 237, 50 g
Light Pink 252, 50 g
Beige 249, 50 g

Tunisian Crochet Hook: U.S. size J-10 / 6 mm
Crochet Hook: U.S. size G-6 / 4 mm for
foundation chain and edging

GAUGE:
20 sts in Tunisian crochet pattern
with larger hook = 4 in / 10 cm.
Adjust hook size to obtain correct gauge if
necessary.

1 pattern repeat = 2 sts

Tunisian Crochet Stitches Used: Vertical stitch
and twisted vertical stitch (see pages 122-123).
Crochet Stitches Used: Chain st (ch) and slip st
(sl st) (see page 110).

Change colors on the return row, on the last
step of the stitch just before the first new color
stitch in Tunisian crochet. See page 124 for
step-by-step instructions for changing colors.
Using this method produces a "whole color" on
the 1st st of the forward row.

Carry the color not in use for a row up the side.

Hand Towel

INSTRUCTIONS:

With smaller size hook and Gray-Purple, ch 62 sts.

Row 1, forward: Change to Tunisian crochet hook and begin in the 2nd ch from hook. Pick up 61 vertical sts in the top loop of each chain = 62 loops on the hook.

Row 1, return: Bind off each stitch as follows: Yarn around hook and through the first loop on the hook, *yarn around hook and through 2 loops on hook*; rep * to * across.

Row 2, forward: 1 edge st, pick up *1 vertical loop, 1 twisted vertical loop*; rep from * to * across, ending with 1 edge st = 62 sts on hook.

Row 2, return: Bind off all sts.

Rows 3-10, forward and return: Work as for Row 2, forward and return.

Row 11, forward: Change to Light Purple, continue in pattern through Row 13, return and then cut yarn.

Row 14, forward: Change to Gray-Purple.

Row 15, forward: Change to Beige; continue in pattern through Row 16, return and then cut yarn.

Row 17, forward: Change to Gray-Purple.

Row 18, forward: Change to Light Pink; cut yarn after return.

Row 19, forward: Change to Gray-Purple and continue in pattern through Row 60, return.

Row 61, forward: Change to Light Pink; cut yarn after return.

Row 62, forward: Change to Gray-Purple.

Row 63, forward: Change to Beige; cut yarn after Row 64, return.

Row 65, forward: Change to Gray-Purple.

Row 66, forward: Change to Light Purple, continue in pattern through Row 68, return and then cut yarn.

Row 69, forward: Change to Gray-Purple.

Rows 70-71, forward and return: Work as for Row 2, forward and return.

Row 72, forward: Work to the center of the piece and back to form the hanging loop as follows: 1 edge st, pick up (1 vertical st, 1 twisted vertical st) 15 times and end with 1 vertical st = 31 loops on hook.

Row 72, return: Bind off all sts as follows: *Yarn around hook, bring through 2 loops*; rep * to * across.

Row 73, forward: 1 edge st, pick up (1 vertical st, 1 twisted vertical st) 15 times and end with 1 vertical st = 31 loops on hook.

Row 73, return: Bind off all sts as follows: Yarn around hook and through 1 st, *yarn around hook, bring through 2 loops*; rep * to across.

Rows 74-76, forward and return: Work as for Row 73, forward and return.

Row 77, forward: 1 edge st, pick up (1 vertical st, 1 twisted vertical st) 15 times and end with 1 vertical st = 31 loops on hook. Cut yarn, leaving a long tail to use for reinforcing the hanging loop later. Leave sts on hook.

Repeat the sequence beginning at Row 73, forward, on the other half of the towel; this time, on Row 77, forward, do not cut yarn. Continue as follows:

Row 77, return: Bind off all the sts on the hook (including those of the first half of the opening) as follows: Yarn around hook and through 1 st, *yarn around hook, bring through 2 loops*; rep * to across.

Rows 78-79, forward and return: Work as for Row 2, forward and return. With smaller size hook, bind off with chain and slip sts: Insert hook through *2 sts and join them with 1 sl st, ch 1*; rep * to * across, ending with 1 sl st in the edge st. Do not cut yarn, but, instead, continue around with the edging, beginning on the 1st long side.

Edging: With smaller hook, work 1 sl st in corner, work 1 sl st in each st along edge, 1 sl st in corner and then continue along the foundation chain with 1 sl st in each ch; 1 sl st in corner and then 1 sl st in each st along last long side; end with 1 sl st in the 1st sl st; cut yarn.

FINISHING:

Weave in all ends neatly. Lightly steam press the towel on the wrong side to finished measurements.

Potholder

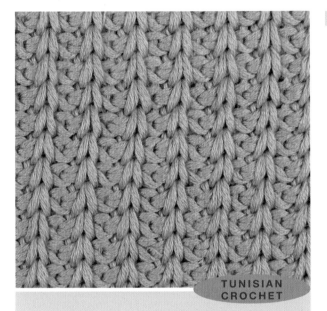

TUNISIAN CROCHET

MEASUREMENTS:
Approx. 8 x 8 in / 20 x 20 cm

MATERIALS:
Yarn: CYCA #4, PT Sumatra (100% pima cotton, 93 yd/85 m / 50 g)
Pink 3027, 100 g

Tunisian Crochet Hook: U.S. size K-10½ / 6.5 mm
Crochet Hook: U.S. size H-8 / 5 mm for foundation chain and edging

GAUGE:
18 sts in Tunisian crochet pattern
with larger hook = 4 in / 10 cm.
Adjust hook size to obtain correct gauge if necessary.

1 pattern repeat = 2 sts

Tunisian Crochet Stitches Used: Vertical stitch and twisted vertical stitch (see pages 122-123).
Crochet Stitches Used: Chain st (ch) and slip st (sl st) (see page 110).

INSTRUCTIONS:
With smaller size hook, ch 36 sts.

Row 1, forward: Change to Tunisian crochet hook and begin in the 2nd ch from hook. Pick up 35 vertical sts in the top loop of each chain = 36 loops on the hook.

Row 1, return: Bind off each stitch as follows: Yarn around hook and through the first loop on the hook, *yarn around hook and through 2 loops on hook*; rep * to * across.

Row 2, forward: 1 edge st, pick up *1 vertical st, 1 twisted vertical st*; rep * to * across, ending with 1 edge st = 36 loops on hook.

Row 2, return: Bind off all sts.

Rows 3-29, forward and return (or until potholder is squared): Work as for Row 2, forward and return. Change to smaller size hook and finish with chain and slip sts as follows: Insert hook through *2 sts and join them with 1 sl st, ch 1*; rep * to * across, ending with 1 sl st in the edge st. Do not cut yarn, but, instead, continue around with the edging.

Edging: With smaller hook, work 1 sl st in corner, work 1 sl st in each st along edge, 1 sl st in corner and then along the foundation chain with 1 sl st in each ch; 1 sl st in corner and then 1 sl st in each st along last long side; end with hanging loop at corner: ch 12 and attach loop to beg of rnd with 1 sl st and then 1 sl st in the 1st sl st; cut yarn.

Make a second potholder the same way.

FINISHING:
Weave in all ends neatly. Lightly steam press the potholder on the wrong side to finished measurements.

Flower Potholder

CROCHET

MEASUREMENTS:
Approx. 8¼ in / 21 cm in diameter

MATERIALS:
Yarn: CYCA #2, PT Petunia (100% pima cotton, 120 yd/110 m / 50 g)
Purple 250, 50 g
Light Purple 237, 50 g

Crochet Hook: U.S. size D-3 / 3.25 mm

GAUGE:
22 sts = 4 in / 10 cm.
Adjust hook size to obtain correct gauge if necessary.

Crochet Stitches Used: Chain st (ch), slip st (sl st), single crochet (sc), double crochet (dc) (see pages 110-113).

( ) Repeat the sequence within parentheses the number of times specified after the end parenthesis.

INSTRUCTIONS:
With Purple, ch 4 and join into a ring with 1 sl st into 1st ch.

Rnd 1: Ch 1, work 8 sc around ring, and end with 1 sl st into 1st ch = 8 sc.

Rnd 2: Ch 1, *1 sc in next sc, 2 sc in next sc*; rep * to * around, ending with 1 sl st into 1st ch = 12 sc.

Rnd 3: Ch 1, *1 sc in next sc, 2 sc in next sc*; rep * to * around, ending with 1 sl st into 1st ch = 18 sc.

Rnd 4: Ch 1, *(1 sc in next sc) 2 times, 2 sc in next sc*; rep * to * around, ending with 1 sl st into 1st ch = 24 sc. Change to Light Purple on last step of final st.

Rnd 5: With Light Purple, ch 3 (= 1st dc), ch 1, 1 dc in the same sc, *ch 1, skip 1 sc, 1 dc in next sc, ch 1, 1 dc in same sc*; rep * to * around, ending with ch 1, 1 sl st into top of ch 3.

Rnd 6: 1 sl st around ch, ch 3 (= 1st dc), 1 dc around same ch loop, ch 2, 2 dc around same ch loop, *ch 1, skip (1 dc, ch 1, 1 dc), 2 dc around ch loop, ch 2, 2 dc around same ch loop *; rep * to * around, ending with ch 1, 1 sl st into top of ch 3.

Rnd 7: 1 sl st in dc, 1 sl st around ch loop, ch 3 (= 1st dc), 2 dc around same ch loop, ch 2, 3 dc around same ch loop, *ch 1, skip (2 dc, ch 1, 2 dc), 3 dc around ch loop, ch 2, 3 dc around same ch loop*; rep * to * around, ending with ch 1, 1 sl st into top of ch 3.

Rnd 8: (1 sl st in dc) 2 times, 1 sl st around ch loop, ch 3 (= 1st dc), 2 dc around same ch loop, ch 2, 3 dc around same ch loop, *ch 1, skip (3 dc, ch 1, 3 dc), 3 dc around ch loop, ch 2, 3 dc around same ch loop*; rep * to * around, ending with ch 1, 1 sl st into top of ch 3.

Rnd 9: (1 sl st in dc) 2 times, 1 sl st around ch loop, ch 3 (= 1st dc), 3 dc around same ch loop, ch 2, 4 dc around same ch loop, *ch 1, skip (3 dc, ch 1, 3 dc), 4 dc around ch loop, ch 2, 4 dc around same ch loop*; rep * to * around, ending with ch 1, 1 sl st into top of ch 3.

Rnd 10: (1 sl st in dc) 3 times, 1 sl st around ch loop, ch 3 (= 1st dc), 9 dc around same ch loop, *ch 1, skip (4 dc, ch 1, 4 dc), 10 dc around ch loop*; rep * to * around, ending with ch 1, 1 sl st into top of ch 3. Cut yarn.

Edging: Attach Purple with 1 sl st into 1st dc of round. Ch 1, *(1 sc in next dc) 2 times, (2 sc in same dc, 1 sc in next dc) 3 times, 1 sc in dc, 1 sc around ch loop, ch 1; turn work with fan towards you, ch 1, 1 sl st around ch of 9th rnd, ch 1, 1 sl st around ch of 8th rnd, ch 1, 1 sl st around ch of 7th rnd, ch 1, 1 sl st around ch of 6th rnd, ch 1, 1 sl st around ch of 5th rnd, ch 1, 1 sl st in sc of 4th rnd; turn. Ch 1, 1 sl st around ch of 5th rnd, ch 1, 1 sl st around ch of 6th rnd, ch 1, 1 sl st around ch of 7th rnd, ch 1, 1 sl st around ch of 8th rnd, ch 1, 1 sl st around ch of 9th rnd, ch 1, 1 sl st around ch of 10th rnd, ch 1*; rep from * to * around, ending with 1 sl st into 1st sc. Do not cut yarn. Work hanging loop: ch 12 and attach loop with 1 sl st into base of last fan of the round.
Make a second potholder the same way.

FINISHING:
Weave in all ends neatly and gently steam press potholder to finished measurements.

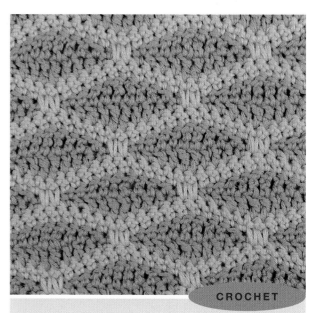

CROCHET

MEASUREMENTS:
Approx. 12¾ x 16 in / 32 x 41 cm

MATERIALS:
Yarn: CYCA #1, Sandnes Garn Mandarin Petit
(100% cotton, 195 yd/178 m / 50 g)
Khaki 2205, 50 g
Light Heather 4622, 50 g

Crochet Hook: U.S. size D-3 / 3.25 mm;
U.S. size E-4 / 3.5 for foundation chain

GAUGE:
2 pattern repeats (= 24 sc) with smaller size
hook = 4 in / 10 cm.
Adjust hook size to obtain correct gauge if
necessary.

1 pattern repeat = 12 sts

Crochet Stitches Used: Chain st (ch), slip st
(sl st), single crochet (sc), half double crochet
(hdc), double crochet (dc), treble crochet (tr)
(see pages 110-113).

( ) Repeat the sequence within parentheses
the number of times specified after the end
parenthesis.

When changing colors, bring new color through
on the last step of the last st of the previous
row. This produces a "complete" color on the
first st of the next row.

Carry the color not in use for a row up the side.

Brick Pattern Hand Towel

With larger size hook and Khaki, ch 73.

Row 1: Change to smaller size hook. Beg in 2nd ch from hook, work 1 sc in each ch across = 72 sc; turn.

Row 2: Ch 1, work 1 sc in each sc across; turn.

Row 3: Change to Light Heather, ch 4 (= 1 tr), (1 dc in sc) 2 times, 1 hdc in sc, 1 sc in sc, *ch 2, skip 2 sc, 1 sc in sc, 1 hdc in sc, (1 dc in sc) 2 times, (1 tr in sc) 2 times, (1 dc in sc) 2 times, 1 hdc in sc, 1 sc in sc*; rep from * to * across, ending with ch 2, skip 2 sc, 1 sc in sc, 1 hdc in sc, (1 dc in sc) 2 times, 1 tr in sc; turn.

Row 4: Ch 4 (= 1 tr), (1 dc in dc) 2 times, 1 hdc in hdc, 1 sc in sc, *ch 2, skip 2 ch, 1 sc in sc, 1 hdc in hdc, (1 dc in dc) 2 times, (1 tr in tr) 2 times, (1 dc in dc) 2 times, 1 hdc in hdc, 1 sc in sc*; rep from * to * across, ending with ch 2, skip 2 ch, 1 sc in sc, 1 hdc in hdc, (1 dc in dc) 2 times, 1 tr in 4th ch; turn.

Row 5: Change to Khaki, ch 1, 1 sc in tr, (1 sc in dc) 2 times, 1 sc in hdc, 1 sc in sc, *1 sc in sc on 2nd row 2 times (= a stretched stitch that is worked around the ch loops of the 3rd and 4th rows that will lie flat and be hidden in the sc), 1 sc in sc, 1 sc in hdc, (1 sc in dc) 2 times, (1 sc in tr) 2 times, (1 sc in dc) 2 times, 1 sc in hdc, 1 sc in sc*; rep from * to * across, ending with (1 sc in sc on 2nd row) 2 times, 1 sc in sc, 1 sc in hdc, (1 sc in dc) 2 times, 1 sc in 4th ch; turn.

Row 6: Ch 1, 1 sc in each sc across; turn.

Row 7: Change to Light Heather. Ch 1, 1 sc in sc, *1 sc in sc, 1 hdc in sc, (1 dc in sc) 2 times, (1 tr in sc) 2 times, (1 dc in sc) 2 times, 1 hdc, in sc, 1 sc in sc, ch 2, skip 2 sc*; rep from * to * across, ending with 1 sc in sc, 1 hdc in sc, (1 dc in sc) 2 times, (1 tr in sc) 2 times, (1 dc in sc) 2 times, 1 hdc, in sc, (1 sc in sc) 2 times; turn.

Row 8: Ch 1, 1 sc in sc, *1 sc in sc, 1 hdc in hdc, (1 dc in dc) 2 times, (1 tr in tr) 2 times, (1 dc in dc) 2 times, 1 hdc in hdc, 1 sc in sc, ch 2, skip 2 ch*; rep from * to * across, ending with 1 sc in sc, 1 hdc in hdc, (1 dc in dc) 2 times, (1 tr in tr) 2 times, (1 dc in dc) 2 times, 1 hdc in hdc, (1 sc in sc) 2 times; turn.

Row 9: Change to Khaki, ch 1, 1 sc in sc, *1 sc in sc, 1 sc in hdc, (1 sc in dc) 2 times, (1 sc in tr) 2 times, (1 sc in dc) 2 times, 1 sc in hdc, 1 sc in sc, (1 sc in sc of Row 6) 2 times*; rep from * to * across, ending with 1 sc in sc, 1 sc in hdc, (1 sc in dc) 2 times, (1 sc in tr) 2 times, (1 sc in dc) 2 times, 1 sc in hdc, (1 sc in sc) 2 times; turn.

Row 10: Ch 1, 1 sc in each sc across; turn.
Repeat Rows 3-10 until the piece measures approx. 15½ in / 39 cm or desired length. End with Rows 3-5. This time, work Row 6 as follows: work (1 sc in sc) 29 times, ch 9 (= hanging loop), skip 5 sc, 1 sc in next sc, continue across with 1 sc in each sc to end of row.

Edging: Continue with Khaki, working 1 sc in each sc up to the hanging loop; work 10 sc around ch loop (= hanging loop), and then work 1 sc in each sc to corner. Work 2 sc in corner. Continue in sc down long side, with 1 sc in each row, 2 sc in next corner, 1 sc in each chain along foundation chain, 2 sc in corner, and 1 sc in each row up other long side. End with 1 sl st into 1st sc. Cut yarn.

Weave in all ends neatly and gently steam press towel to finished measurements.

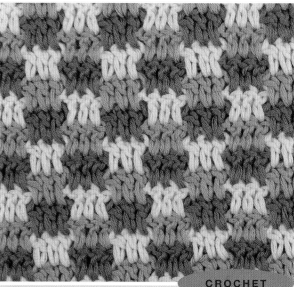

MEASUREMENTS:
Approx. 11½ x 16 in / 29 x 41 cm

MATERIALS:
Yarn: CYCA #1, Sandnes Garn Mandarin Petit
(100% cotton, 195 yd/178 m / 50 g)
Natural White 1002, 50 g
Khaki 2205, 50 g
Heather 4853, 50 g

Crochet Hook: U.S. size D-3 / 3.25 mm;
U.S. size E-4 / 3.5 for foundation chain

GAUGE:
3.5 pattern repeats (= 21 sts) with smaller
size hook = 4 in / 10 cm.
Adjust hook size to obtain correct gauge if
necessary.

1 pattern repeat = 6 sts

Crochet Stitches Used: Chain st (ch), slip st
(sl st), single crochet (sc), half double crochet
(hdc), double crochet (dc) (see pages 110-113).

( ) Repeat the sequence within parentheses
the number of times specified after the end
parenthesis.

When changing colors, bring new color through
on the last step of the last st of the previous
row. This produces a "complete" color on the
first st of the next row.

Carry the color not in use for a row up the side.

Stair Step Pattern Hand Towel

INSTRUCTIONS:

With larger size hook and Natural White, ch 66.

Row 1: Change to smaller hook. Beg in 4th ch from hook, work (1 dc in ch) 2 times, *ch 3, skip 3 ch, (1 dc in next ch) 3 times*; rep from * to * across; turn.

Row 2: Change to Beige. Ch 3, *skip 3 dc, 3 dc around both ch loops (= around the foundation chain and ch from Row 1), ch 3*; rep from * to * across, ending with 1 sl st into top of ch 3.

Row 3: Change to Heather. Ch 3, (1 dc in dc 2 rows below at the same time as working around ch from previous row; the chain will now be hidden) 2 times, *ch 3, skip 3 dc, (1 dc in dc 2 rows below while also crocheting over the loop of previous row) 3 times*; rep from * to * across; turn.

Row 4: Change to Natural White. Ch 3, *skip 3 dc, (1 dc in dc 2 rows below while also crocheting over the ch from previous row) 3 times, ch 3*; rep from * to * across, ending with 1 sl st into top of ch 3; turn.

Row 5: Change to Beige. Ch 3, (1 dc in dc 2 rows below at the same time as working around ch from previous row; the chain will now be hidden) 2 times, *ch 3, skip 3 dc, (1 dc in dc 2 rows below while also crocheting over the loop of previous row) 3 times*; rep from * to * across; turn.

Row 6: Change to Heather. Ch 3, *skip 3 dc, (1 dc in dc 2 rows below while also crocheting over the ch from previous row) 3 times, ch 3*; rep from * to * across, ending with 1 sl st into top of ch 3; turn.

Continue in pattern by repeating Rows 5 and 6 until piece measures approx. 16 in / 41 cm long. *At the same time*, change colors on every row as follows: Natural White, Beige, Heather. End with Row 6; turn.

Edging: With Beige, continue along top edge. Ch 2, (1 hdc in dc 2 row below, at the same time crocheting over the ch from previous row—the ch will be covered) 2 times, *(1 sc in dc) 3 times, (1 hdc in dc 2 rows below, at the same time crocheting over ch from previous row) 3 times*; rep from * to * across, **BUT**, when 4 sts past the center of the towel, ch 12 (= hanging loop), skip 8 sts back on the row and attach hanging loop with a sl st into sc; turn and work 15 sc around loop. Continue across as before, working 2 sc in corner. Work down the long side with 1 sc in each row, 2 sc in next corner, and then 1 sc in each ch along foundation ch; 2 sc in corner and then 1 sc in each row up long side. End with 1 sl st to 1st sc. Cut yarn.

FINISHING:

Weave in all ends neatly and gently steam press towel to finished measurements.

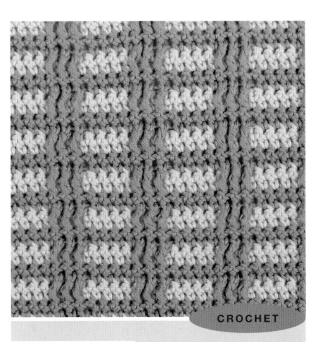

CROCHET

MEASUREMENTS:
Approx. 12¾ x 17¾ in / 32 x 45 cm

MATERIALS:
Yarn: CYCA #1, PT Pandora (100% pima cotton, 180 yd/165 m / 50 g)
Light Beige 238, 50 g
Sand 236, 100 g

Crochet Hook: U.S. size D-3 / 3.25 mm;
U.S. size E-4 / 3.5 mm for foundation chain

GAUGE:
3.5 pattern repeats (= 21 sts) in pattern with smaller hook = 4 in / 10 cm.
Adjust hook size to obtain correct gauge if necessary.

1 pattern repeat = 7 sts

Crochet Stitches Used: Chain st (ch), slip st (sl st), single crochet (sc), treble crochet relief st (see pages 110-116).

( ) Repeat the sequence within parentheses the number of times specified after the end parenthesis.

When changing colors, bring new color through on the last step of the last st of the previous row. This produces a "complete" color on the first st of the next row.

Carry the color not in use for a row up the side.

Relief Stitch Hand Towel

With larger size hook and Sand, ch 67 sts.

Row 1: Change to smaller size hook. Beginning in the 2nd ch from hook, work 1 sc in each ch across; turn.
Row 2: Ch 1, work 1 sc in each sc across; turn.
Row 3: Change to Light Beige. Ch 1, work 1 sc in each sc across; turn.
Row 4: Ch 1, work 1 sc in each sc across; turn.
Row 5: Change to Sand. Ch 1, (1 treble relief st around Sand sc 3 rows below) 3 times, *(1 sc in next sc) 4 times, (1 treble relief st around Sand sc 3 rows below) 3 times*; rep * to * across; turn.
Row 6: Ch 1, (1 sc in tr relief st) 3 times, *(1 sc in next sc) 4 times, (1 sc in tr relief st) 3 times*; rep * to * across; turn.
Row 7: Change to Light Beige. Ch 1, 1 sc in each sc across; turn.
Row 8: Ch 1, 1 sc in each sc across; turn.
Row 9: Change to Sand. Ch 1, (1 treble relief st around Sand sc 3 rows below) 3 times, *(1 sc in next sc) 4 times, (1 treble relief st around Sand sc 3 rows below) 3 times*; rep * to * across; turn.
Row 10: Ch 1, (1 sc in tr relief st) 3 times, *(1 sc in next sc) 4 times, (1 sc in tr relief st) 3 times*; rep * to * across; turn.
Repeat Rows 7-10 throughout until piece is approx. 17¾ in / 45 cm long, ending with Row 10.
Edging: Continue with Sand. Ch 1, (1 sc in next sc) 29 times, ch 12 (= hanging loop, skip 7 sc, 1 sc in next sc; turn and work 15 sc over ch for hanging loop, 1 sl st into sc; turn with 1 sl st in each sc back to base of loop and then continue with 1 sc in each sc to corner. Work 2 sc in corner st and then continue down long side with 1 sc in each row; 2 sc in next corner; 1 sc in each ch along foundation chain, 2 sc in corner, and then 1 sc in each row along opposite long side. End with 1 sl st into 1st sc. Cut yarn.

Weave in all ends neatly and gently steam press towel to finished measurements.

Placemat

CROCHET

MEASUREMENTS:
17 x 13½ in / 43 x 34 cm

MATERIALS:
Yarn: CYCA #3, Marks & Kattens M&K Linen
(100% linen, 136 yd/124 m / 50 g)
Light Gray 967, 100 g
Blue 957, 50 g
Dark Blue 963, 50 g

Crochet Hook: U.S. size D-3 / 3.25 mm;
U.S. size E-4 / 3.5 mm for foundation chain

GAUGE:
5 pattern repeats (= 20 sts) in pattern with
smaller hook = 4 in / 10 cm.
Adjust hook size to obtain correct gauge if
necessary.

1 pattern repeat = 4 sts

Crochet Stitches Used: Chain st (ch), slip st
(sl st), single crochet (sc), double crochet (dc)
(see pages 110-113).

( ) Repeat the sequence within parentheses
the number of times specified after the end
parenthesis.

When changing colors between rounds, cut the
old color and weave in the end through back
loops of stitches on WS (see page 114).

INSTRUCTIONS:
With larger size hook and Light Gray, ch 27 sts.
Rnd 1: Change to smaller size hook. Beg in 4th ch
from hook, work 2 dc, ch 3, 3 dc in same ch =
1st part of the corner, ch 1, (skip 3 ch, 3 dc into
same ch, ch 1) 5 times. Skip 3 ch, (3 dc, ch 3,
3 dc, ch 3, 3 dc) in same ch = 2nd corner). Now
work on the opposite side of foundation chain.
Ch 1, (skip 3 ch, 3 dc in same dc as dc group on
opposite side, ch 1); 5 times, skip 3 dc, work 3 dc
in same ch as 1st part of corner, ch 3. End round
with 1 sl st into top of ch 3.
Rnd 2: (1 sl st into dc) 2 times, 1 sl st around ch
loop, ch 3, (2 dc, ch 3, 3 dc) around ch loop, ch
1, (skip 3-dc group, 3 dc around ch loop, ch 1) 6
times; (3 dc, ch 3, 3 dc) around next ch loop =
corner. Ch 1, (3 dc, ch 3, 3 dc) around next ch
loop = corner, ch 1. (Skip 3-dc group, 3 dc around
ch loop, ch 1) 6 times, (3 dc, ch 3, 3 dc) around
next ch loop = corner, ch 1. End with 1 sl st into
top of ch 3.
Rnd 3: (1 sl st into dc) 2 times, 1 sl st around ch
loop, ch 3, (2 dc, ch 3, 3 dc) around ch loop, ch
1, (skip 3-dc group, 3 dc around ch loop, ch 1)
7 times; (3 dc, ch 3, 3 dc) around next ch loop
= corner. Ch 1, skip 3-dc group, 3 dc around ch
loop, ch 1, (3 dc, ch 3, 3 dc) around next ch loop
= corner, ch 1. (Skip 3-dc group, 3 dc around
ch loop, ch 1) 7 times, (3 dc, ch 3, 3 dc) around
next ch loop = corner, ch 1, skip 3-dc group, 3 dc
around ch loop, ch 1. End with 1 sl st into top of
ch 3.
Rnd 4: (1 sl st into dc) 2 times, 1 sl st around ch
loop, ch 3, (2 dc, ch 3, 3 dc) around ch loop, ch
1, (skip 3-dc group, 3 dc around ch loop, ch 1)
8 times; (3 dc, ch 3, 3 dc) around next ch loop
= corner. Ch 1, skip 3-dc group, 3 dc around ch
loop, ch 1, (3 dc, ch 3, 3 dc) around next ch loop
= corner, ch 1. (Skip 3-dc group, 3 dc around
ch loop, ch 1) 2 times, (3 dc, ch 3, 3 dc) around
next ch loop = corner, ch 1, (skip 3-dc group, 3
dc around ch loop, ch 1) 8 times. (3 dc, ch 3, 3
dc) around next ch loop = corner, ch 1, (skip 3-dc
group, 3 dc around ch loop, ch 1) 2 times. End
with 1 sl st into top of ch 3.

Rnd 5: (1 sl st into dc) 2 times, 1 sl st around ch loop, ch 3, (2 dc, ch 3, 3 dc) around ch loop, ch 1, (skip 3-dc group, 3 dc around ch loop, ch 1) 9 times; (3 dc, ch 3, 3 dc) around next ch loop = corner. Ch 1, (skip 3-dc group, 3 dc around ch loop, ch 1) 3 times, (3 dc, ch 3, 3 dc) around next ch loop = corner, ch 1, (skip 3-dc group, 3 dc around ch loop, ch 1) 9 times. (3 dc, ch 3, 3 dc) around next ch loop = corner, ch 1, (skip 3-dc group, 3 dc around ch loop, ch 1) 3 times. End with 1 sl st into top of ch 3.

Rnd 6: (1 sl st into dc) 2 times, 1 sl st around ch loop, ch 3, (2 dc, ch 3, 3 dc) around ch loop, ch 1, (skip 3-dc group, 3 dc around ch loop, ch 1) 10 times; (3 dc, ch 3, 3 dc) around next ch loop = corner. Ch 1, (skip 3-dc group, 3 dc around ch loop, ch 1) 4 times, (3 dc, ch 3, 3 dc) around next ch loop = corner, ch 1, (skip 3-dc group, 3 dc around ch loop, ch 1) 10 times. (3 dc, ch 3, 3 dc) around next ch loop = corner, ch 1, (skip 3-dc group, 3 dc around ch loop, ch 1) 4 times. End with 1 sl st into top of ch 3.

Rnd 7: (1 sl st into dc) 2 times, 1 sl st around ch loop, ch 3, (2 dc, ch 3, 3 dc) around ch loop, ch 1, (skip 3-dc group, 3 dc around ch loop, ch 1) 11 times; (3 dc, ch 3, 3 dc) around next ch loop = corner. Ch 1, (skip 3-dc group, 3 dc around ch loop, ch 1) 5 times, (3 dc, ch 3, 3 dc) around next ch loop = corner, ch 1, (skip 3-dc group, 3 dc around ch loop, ch 1) 11 times. (3 dc, ch 3, 3 dc) around next ch loop = corner, ch 1, (skip 3-dc group, 3 dc around ch loop, ch 1) 5 times. End with 1 sl st into top of ch 3.

Rnd 8: (1 sl st into dc) 2 times, 1 sl st around ch loop, ch 3, (2 dc, ch 3, 3 dc) around ch loop, ch 1, (skip 3-dc group, 3 dc around ch loop, ch 1) 12 times; (3 dc, ch 3, 3 dc) around next ch loop = corner. Ch 1, (skip 3-dc group, 3 dc around ch loop, ch 1) 6 times, (3 dc, ch 3, 3 dc) around next ch loop = corner, ch 1, (skip 3-dc group, 3 dc around ch loop, ch 1) 12 times. (3 dc, ch 3, 3 dc) around next ch loop = corner, ch 1, (skip 3-dc group, 3 dc around ch loop, ch 1) 6 times. End with 1 sl st into top of ch 3.

Rnds 9-13: Continue as set with 1 more dc-group on each of the 4 sides on every rnd. On Rnd 13, cut yarn and weave in along back loops (see page 114).

Rnd 14: Change to Blue, attaching yarn with 1 sc around a corner ch, ch 3, (2 dc, ch 3, 3 dc) around ch loop, ch 1, (skip 3-dc group, 3 dc around ch loop, ch 1) 18 times; (3 dc, ch 3, 3 dc) around next ch loop = corner. Ch 1, (skip 3-dc group, 3 dc around ch loop, ch 1) 12 times, (3 dc, ch 3, 3 dc) around next ch loop = corner, ch 1, (skip 3-dc group, 3 dc around ch loop, ch 1) 18 times. (3 dc, ch 3, 3 dc) around next ch loop = corner, ch 1, (skip 3-dc group, 3 dc around ch loop, ch 1) 12 times. End with 1 sl st into top of ch 3.

Rnd 15: (1 sl st into dc) 2 times, 1 sl st around ch loop, ch 3, (2 dc, ch 3, 3 dc) around ch loop, ch 1, (skip 3-dc group, 3 dc around ch loop, ch 1) 19 times; (3 dc, ch 3, 3 dc) around next ch loop = corner. Ch 1, (skip 3-dc group, 3 dc around ch loop, ch 1) 13 times, (3 dc, ch 3, 3 dc) around next ch loop = corner, ch 1, (skip 3-dc group, 3 dc around ch loop, ch 1) 19 times. (3 dc, ch 3, 3 dc) around next ch loop = corner, ch 1, (skip 3-dc group, 3 dc around ch loop, ch 1) 13 times. End with 1 sl st into top of ch 3.

Cut yarn and weave in along back loops.

Rnd 16: Change to Dark Blue, attaching yarn with 1 sc around a corner ch, ch 3, (2 dc, ch 3, 3 dc) around ch loop, ch 1, (skip 3-dc group, 3 dc around ch loop, ch 1) 20 times; (3 dc, ch 3, 3 dc) around next ch loop = corner. Ch 1, (skip 3-dc group, 3 dc around ch loop, ch 1) 14 times, (3 dc, ch 3, 3 dc) around next ch loop = corner, ch 1, (skip 3-dc group, 3 dc around ch loop, ch 1) 20 times. (3 dc, ch 3, 3 dc) around next ch loop = corner, ch 1, (skip 3-dc group, 3 dc around ch loop, ch 1) 14 times. End with 1 sl st into top of ch 3.

Rnd 17: (1 sl st into dc) 2 times, 4 sc at corner, *(1 sc in next dc) 3 times, 1 sc around ch*; rep * to * to the next corner, (1 sc in next dc) 3 times, 4 sc at corner; rep from * to * to next corner, (1 sc in next dc) 3 times, 4 sc at corner. Work the other two sides as for the first 2 sides and end with 1 sl st into 1st sc.

FINISHING:

Weave in all ends neatly and gently steam press towel to finished measurements.

Natural and Multicolor
Placemat

CROCHET

MEASUREMENTS:
Approx. 17 x 13½ in / 43 x 34 cm

MATERIALS:
Yarn: CYCA #3, Marks & Kattens M&K Linen
(100% linen, 136 yd/124 m / 50 g)
Natural 952, 100 g
Light Purple 961, 50 g
Dark Purple 959, 50 g
Brown 966, 50 g

Crochet Hook: U.S. size D-3 / 3.25 mm;
U.S. size E-4 / 3.5 mm for foundation chain

GAUGE:
8 pattern repeats (= 32 sts) in pattern with
smaller hook = 4 in / 10 cm.
Adjust hook size to obtain correct gauge if
necessary.

1 pattern repeat = 4 sts

Crochet Stitches Used: Chain st (ch), slip st
(sl st), single crochet (sc), double crochet (dc),
crab st (see pages 110-113).

( ) Repeat the sequence within parentheses
the number of times specified after the end
parenthesis.

Tip: When changing colors between rounds,
cut the old color and weave in the end through
back loops of stitches on WS (see step-by-step
photos on page 114).

INSTRUCTIONS:
With larger size hook and Light Purple, ch 20 sts.
Rnd 1: Change to Natural and smaller size hook;
ch 3 as a continuation of the foundation chain.
Beginning in 4th ch from hook, (= 1st dc), work (2
dc, ch 1, 3 dc) in the same ch = first part of the
corner, ch 1, (skip 3 ch, 3 dc in same ch, ch 1)
4 times. Skip 3 ch, (3 dc, ch 1, 3 dc, ch 1, 3 dc)
in same ch = 2nd corner. Now continue on the
opposite side of the foundation chain: Ch 1, (skip
3 ch, 3 dc in same st as a 3-dc group on opposite
side of foundation chain) 4 times, skip 3 ch, 3 dc
in same ch as first part of 1st corner, ch 1; end
rnd with 1 sl st into top of ch 3. Cut yarn and fasten off (see Tip).
Rnd 2: With Dark Purple, attach yarn with 1
sc around ch 1 at corner, ch 3, skip 3 dc, 1 sc
around next corner ch, ch 3, 1 sc around same
corner ch, (ch 3, skip 3 dc, 1 sc around ch) 5
times, ch 3, skip 3 dc, 1 sc around corner ch,
ch 3, 1 sc around same ch, ch 3, skip 3 dc, 1 sc
around next corner ch, ch 3, 1 sc around same
corner ch, (ch 3, skip 3 dc, 1 sc around ch) 5
times, ch 3, skip 3 dc, 1 sc around corner ch, ch
3. End rnd with 1 sl st into 1st sc. Cut yarn and
fasten off.
Rnd 3: With Natural, attach yarn with 1 sl st
around corner ch, ch 3, (2 dc, ch 1, 3 dc) in same
ch loop, ch 1, 3 dc around ch-3 loop, ch 1, skip 1
sc, 3 dc around next corner ch, ch 1, 3 dc around
same corner ch loop, (ch 1, skip 1 sc, 3 dc around
ch loop) 6 times, ch 1. **Skip 1 sc, 3 dc around
corner ch loop, ch 1, 3 dc around same corner
ch loop,** ch 1, skip 1 sc, 3 dc around ch-3 loop,
ch 1, skip 1 sc; rep ** to ** in the next corner ch
loop, (ch 1, skip 1 sc, 3 dc around ch-3 loop) 6
times, ch 1. End rnd with 1 st st into top of ch 3
at beginning of rnd. Cut yarn and fasten off.
Rnd 4: With Brown, attach yarn with 1 sc around
corner ch, ch 3, 1 sc in same ch loop, ch 3, (skip
3 dc, 1 sc around next ch, ch 3) 2 times, skip 3
dc, 1 sc around next corner ch, ch 3, 1 sc around
same corner ch. (Ch 3, skip 3 dc, 1 sc around ch)
7 times, ch 3, skip 3 dc, 1 sc around next corner
ch, ch 3, 1 sc around same corner ch, ch 3, (skip
3 dc, 1 sc around ch, ch 3) 2 times, skip 3 dc,
1 sc around next corner ch, ch 3, 1 sc around
same corner ch. (Ch 3, skip 3 dc, 1 sc around ch)
7 times. End rnd with ch 3, skip 3 dc, 1 sl st into
1st sc. Cut yarn and fasten off.
Rnd 5: With Natural, attach yarn with 1 sl st
around corner 3-ch loop, ch 3, (2 dc, ch 1, 3 dc)
in same corner ch loop, (ch 1, skip 1 sc, 3 dc
around ch-3 loop) 3 times, ch 1, skip 1 sc, 3 dc

around next corner ch loop, ch 1, 3 dc around same corner ch loop, (ch 1, skip 1 sc, 3 dc around ch-3 loop) 8 times, ch 1. **Skip 1 sc, 3 dc around corner ch loop, ch 1, 3 dc around same corner ch loop**, (ch 1, skip 1 sc, 3 dc around ch-3 loop) 3 times, ch 1, skip 1 sc; rep ** to ** in the next corner ch loop, (ch 1, skip 1 sc, 3 dc around ch-3 loop) 8 times, ch 1. End rnd with 1 st st into top of ch 3 at beginning of rnd. Cut yarn and fasten off.

Rnd 6: With Light Purple, attach yarn with 1 sc around corner ch, ch 3, 1 sc in same ch loop, ch 3, **ch 3, skip 3 dc, 1 sc around next ch) **; rep ** to ** 4 times, ch 3, skip 3 dc, 1 sc around next corner ch, ch 3, 1 sc around same corner ch. (Ch 3, skip 3 dc, 1 sc around ch) 9 times, ch 3, skip 3 dc, 1 sc around next corner ch, ch 3, 1 sc around same corner ch, rep ** to ** 4 times, skip 3 dc, 1 sc around ch, ch 3, 1 sc around next corner ch, ch 3, 1 sc around same corner ch. (Ch 3, skip 3 dc, 1 sc around ch) 9 times, ch 3, skip 3 dc, end rnd with 1 sl st into 1st sc. Cut yarn and fasten off.

Rnd 7: With Natural, attach yarn with 1 sl st around corner ch-3 loop, ch 3, (2 dc, ch 1, 3 dc) in same corner ch loop, (ch 1, skip 1 sc, 3 dc around ch-3 loop) 5 times, ch 1, skip 1 sc, 3 dc around next corner ch loop, ch 1, 3 dc around same corner ch loop, (ch 1, skip 1 sc, 3 dc around ch-3 loop) 10 times, ch 1. **Skip 1 sc, 3 dc around corner ch loop, ch 1, 3 dc around same corner ch loop**, (ch 1, skip 1 sc, 3 dc around ch-3 loop) 5 times, ch 1, skip 1 sc; rep ** to ** in the next corner ch loop, (ch 1, skip 1 sc, 3 dc around ch-3 loop) 10 times, ch 1. End rnd with 1 st st into top of ch 3 at beginning of rnd. Cut yarn and fasten off.

Rnd 8: With Dark Purple, attach yarn with 1 sc around corner ch, ch 3, 1 sc in same ch loop, ch 3, **ch 3, skip 3 dc, 1 sc around next ch **; rep ** to ** 6 times, ch 3, skip 3 dc, 1 sc around next corner ch, ch 3, 1 sc around same corner ch. (Ch 3, skip 3 dc, 1 sc around ch) 11 times, ch 3, skip 3 dc, 1 sc around next corner ch, ch 3, 1 sc around same corner ch, rep ** to ** 6 times, skip 3 dc, 1 sc around ch, ch 3, 1 sc around next corner ch, ch 3, 1 sc around same corner ch. (Ch 3, skip 3 dc, 1 sc around ch) 11 times, ch 3, skip 3 dc, end rnd with 1 sl st into 1st sc. Cut yarn and fasten off.

Rnd 9: With Natural, attach yarn with 1 sl st around corner ch-3 loop, ch 3, (2 dc, ch 1, 3 dc) in same corner ch loop, (ch 1, skip 1 sc, 3 dc around ch-3 loop) 7 times, ch 1, skip 1 sc, 3 dc around next corner ch loop, ch 1, 3 dc around

same corner ch loop, (ch 1, skip 1 sc, 3 dc around ch-3 loop) 12 times, ch 1. **Skip 1 sc, 3 dc around corner ch loop, ch 1, 3 dc around same corner ch loop**, (ch 1, skip 1 sc, 3 dc around ch-3 loop) 7 times, ch 1, skip 1 sc; rep ** to ** in the next corner ch loop, (ch 1, skip 1 sc, 3 dc around ch-3 loop) 12 times, ch 1. End rnd with 1 st st into top of ch 3 at beginning of rnd. Cut yarn and fasten off.

Rnd 10: With Brown, attach yarn with 1 sc around corner ch, ch 3, 1 sc in same ch loop, ch 3, **ch 3, skip 3 dc, 1 sc around next ch **; rep ** to ** 8 times, ch 3, skip 3 dc, 1 sc around next corner ch, ch 3, 1 sc around same corner ch. (Ch 3, skip 3 dc, 1 sc around ch) 13 times, ch 3, skip 3 dc, 1 sc around next corner ch, ch 3, 1 sc around same corner ch, rep ** to ** 8 times, skip 3 dc, 1 sc around ch, ch 3, 1 sc around next corner ch, ch 3, 1 sc around same corner ch. (Ch 3, skip 3 dc, 1 sc around ch) 13 times, ch 3, skip 3 dc, end rnd with 1 sl st into 1st sc. Cut yarn and fasten off.

Rnd 11: With Natural, attach yarn with 1 sl st around corner 3-ch loop, ch 3, (2 dc, ch 1, 3 dc) in same corner ch loop, (ch 1, skip 1 sc, 3 dc around ch-3 loop) 9 times, ch 1, skip 1 sc, 3 dc around next corner ch loop, ch 1, 3 dc around same corner ch loop, (ch 1, skip 1 sc, 3 dc around ch-3 loop) 14 times, ch 1. **Skip 1 sc, 3 dc around corner ch loop, ch 1, 3 dc around same corner ch loop**, (ch 1, skip 1 sc, 3 dc around ch-3 loop) 9 times, ch 1, skip 1 sc; rep ** to ** in the next corner ch loop, (ch 1, skip 1 sc, 3 dc around ch-3 loop) 14 times, ch 1. End rnd with 1 st st into top of ch 3 at beginning of rnd. Cut yarn and fasten off.

Rnd 12: With Brown, attach yarn with 1 sc around corner ch, ch 3, 1 sc in same ch loop, ch 3, **ch 3, skip 3 dc, 1 sc around next ch **; rep ** to ** 10 times, ch 3, skip 3 dc, 1 sc around next corner ch, ch 3, 1 sc around same corner ch. (Ch 3, skip 3 dc, 1 sc around ch) 15 times, ch 3, skip 3 dc, 1 sc around next corner ch, ch 3, 1 sc around same corner ch, rep ** to ** 10 times, skip 3 dc, 1 sc around ch, ch 3, 1 sc around next corner ch, ch 3, 1 sc around same corner ch. (Ch 3, skip 3 dc, 1 sc around ch) 15 times, ch 3, skip 3 dc, end rnd with 1 sl st into 1st sc. Cut yarn and fasten off.

Rnd 13: With Natural, work as for Rnd 11, working each repeat 2 times more.

Rnd 14: With Dark Purple, work as for Rnd 12, working each repeat 2 times more.

Rnd 15: With Natural, work as for Rnd 13, working each repeat 2 times more.

Rnd 16: With Brown, work as for Rnd 14, working each repeat 2 times more.

Rnd 17: With Natural, work as for Rnd 15, working each repeat 2 times more.

Rnd 18: With Light Purple, work as for Rnd 16, working each repeat 2 times more.

Rnd 19: With Natural, work as for Rnd 17, working each repeat 2 times more.

Rnd 20: With Dark Purple, work as for Rnd 18, working each repeat 2 times more.

Rnd 21: With Dark Purple, work as for Rnd 19, working each repeat 2 times more.

Rnd 22: With Dark Purple, work 1 crab st in each dc and ch around; end rnd with 1 sl st into 1st crab st. Cut yarn and fasten off.

FINISHING:

Block placemat to finished measurements; spray to dampen and leave until completely dry.

Handbag and Drawstring Bag

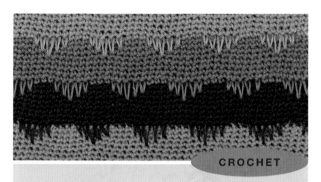

CROCHET

Handbag

MEASUREMENTS:
Length: approx. 14¼ in / 36 cm
Circumference: approx. 26¾ in / 68 cm

MATERIALS:
Yarn: CYCA #3, Marks & Kattens M&K Linen
(100% linen, 136 yd/124 m / 50 g)
Dark Blue 963, 100 g
Blue 957, 50 g
Light Blue 964, 50 g

Notions: Leather handles; waxed linen thread;
stitch marker

Crochet Hook: U.S. size D-3 / 3.25 mm;
U.S. size E-4 / 3.5 mm for foundation chain

GAUGE:
19 sc with smaller hook = 4 in / 10 cm.
Adjust hook size to obtain correct gauge if
necessary.

1 pattern repeat = 8 sts

Crochet Stitches Used: Chain st (ch), slip st
(sl st), single crochet (sc), double crochet (dc),
crab stitch (see pages 110-117).

( ) Repeat the sequence within parentheses
the number of times specified after the end
parenthesis.

When changing colors, bring new color through
on the last step of the last st of the previous
row. This produces a "complete" color on the
first st of the next row.

INSTRUCTIONS FOR HANDBAG:
The handbag is worked from the base up.
With larger size hook and Dark Blue, ch 51 sts.
Rnd 1: Change to smaller hook. Beginning in the
2nd ch from hook, work 4 sc in the same ch and
then work 1 sc in each of the next 48 ch; work 4
sc in last ch. Continue along opposite side of the
foundation chain: work 1 sc in each of next 48
ch; end with 1 sl st into 1st sc = 104 sc around.
Rnd 2: (1 sl st into sc) 2 times, place marker
(move marker up at the same place every round),
ch 1, 2 sc in same sc; work 1 sc in every sc to
the 4-sc-in-1 st on opposite side. Place marker
between the 2 center sc here (the side of the
bag), work 2 sc in the same sc in the last sc
before the marker and repeat this on the first sc
after the marker. Continue with 1 sc in each sc to
the last sc of rnd; work 2 sc in the same sc and
end with 1 sl st into 1st sc = 108 sc around.
Rnd 3: Work as for Rnd 2, increasing 4 sc on the
round = 112 sc.
Rnd 4: Work as for Rnd 3 = 116 sc.
Rnd 5: Work as for Rnd 4 = 120 sc.
Rnd 6: Work as for Rnd 5 = 124 sc.
Rnd 7: Work as for Rnd 6 = 128 sc.
Rnd 8: Work as for Rnd 7 = 132 sc.
Rnd 9: Work as for Rnd 8 = 136 sc.
Rnd 10: Work as for Rnd 9 = 140 sc.
Rnd 11: Work as for Rnd 10 = 144 sc.
Rnd 12: Ch 1, 1 sc in back loop of every sc
around, ending with 1 sl st into 1st ch = 144 sc.
This rnd is the transition between the base and
sides of the bag.
Rnd 13: Ch 1, 1 sc in every sc around, ending
with 1 sl st into 1st ch.
Rnds 14-28: Work as for Rnd 13, changing to Blue
on the last step of the last st on Rnd 28; cut Dark
Blue.
Rnd 29: With Blue, ch 1, *1 long sc in sc 2 rows
below, 1 long sc in sc 3 rows below, 1 long sc in
sc 4 rows below, 1 long sc in sc 3 rows below,
1 long sc in sc 2 rows below, (1 sc in next sc) 3
times*; rep from * to *around, ending with 1 sl st
into 1st ch.
Rnd 30: Ch 1, 1 sc in each sc around, ending with
1 sl st into 1st ch.
Rnds 31-38: Work as for Row 30, changing to
Light Blue on final step of last st of Rnd 38; cut
Blue.
Rnd 39: With Light Blue, ch 1, 1 long sc in sc 2

rows below, *(1 sc in next sc) 3 times, 1 long sc in sc two rows below, 1 long sc in sc 3 rows below, 1 long sc in sc 4 rows below, 1 long sc in sc 3 rows below, 1 long sc in sc 2 rows below*; rep * to * around, ending with (1 sc in next sc) 3 times, 1 long sc in sc two rows below, 1 long sc in sc 3 rows below, 1 long sc in sc 4 rows below, 1 long sc in sc 3 rows below, 1 sl st into 1st ch.

Rnd 40: Ch 1, 1 sc in each sc around, ending with 1 sl st into 1st ch.

Rnds 41-47: Work as for Rnd 40, changing to Dark Blue on final step of last st of Rnd 47; cut Light Blue.

Rnd 48: With Dark Blue, ch 1, *1 long sc in sc 2 rows below, 1 long sc in sc 3 rows below, 1 long sc in sc 4 rows below, 1 long sc in sc 3 rows below, 1 long sc in sc 2 rows below, (1 sc in next sc) 3 times*; rep from * to *around, ending with 1 sl st into 1st ch.

Rnd 49: Ch 1, 1 sc in each sc around, ending with 1 sl st into 1st ch.

Rnds 50-56: Work as for Rnd 49 changing to Blue on final step of last st of Rnd 47; cut Dark Blue.

Rnd 57: With Blue, ch 1, 1 long sc in sc 2 rows below, *(1 sc in next sc) 3 times, 1 long sc in sc two rows below, 1 long sc in sc 3 rows below, 1 long sc in sc 4 rows below, 1 long sc in sc 3 rows below, 1 long sc in sc 2 rows below*; rep * to * around, ending with (1 sc in next sc) 3 times, 1 long sc in sc two rows below, 1 long sc in sc 3 rows below, 1 long sc in sc 4 rows below, 1 long sc in sc 3 rows below, 1 sl st into 1st ch.

Rnd 58: Ch 1, 1 sc in each sc around, ending with 1 sl st into 1st ch.

Rnds 59-65: Work as for Rnd 58, changing to Light Blue on final step of last st of Rnd 65; cut Blue.

Rnd 66: With Light Blue, ch 1, *1 long sc in sc 2 rows below, 1 long sc in sc 3 rows below, 1 long sc in sc 4 rows below, 1 long sc in sc 3 rows below, 1 long sc in sc 2 rows below, (1 sc in next sc) 3 times*; rep from * to *around, ending with 1 sl st into 1st ch.

Rnd 67: Ch 1, 1 sc in each sc around, ending with 1 sl st into 1st ch.

Rnds 68-74: Work as for Rnd 49, changing to Dark Blue on final step of last st of Rnd 74; cut Light Blue.

Rnd 75: With Dark Blue, ch 1, 1 long sc in sc 2 rows below, *(1 sc in next sc) 3 times, 1 long sc in sc two rows below, 1 long sc in sc 3 rows below, 1 long sc in sc 4 rows below, 1 long sc in sc 3 rows below, 1 long sc in sc 2 rows below*; rep * to * around, ending with (1 sc in next sc) 3 times, 1 long sc in sc two rows below, 1 long sc

in sc 3 rows below, 1 long sc in sc 4 rows below, 1 long sc in sc 3 rows below, 1 sl st into 1st ch.

Rnd 76: Ch 1, 1 sc in each sc around, ending with 1 sl st into 1st ch.

Rnds 77-110: Work as for Rnd 76.

Rnd 111: Ch 1, 1 crab st in each sc around, ending with 1 sl st into 1st ch.

FINISHING:

Weave in all ends neatly on WS. Measure or count to the center of each side and place a pin at center points. Center the leather handles at each center pin, with the top of the leather handle ⅜ in / 1 cm down the from the crab st edging. Sew on the handles with waxed linen.

ALTERNATIVE FOR LEATHER HANDLES:

With Dark Blue and larger hook, ch 106.

Row 1: Change to smaller hook. Beginning in 2nd ch from hook, work 1 sc in each ch across = 104 sc. Turn.

Row 2: Ch 1, work 1 sc in each sc across = 104 sc; turn.

Rows 3-10: Work as for Row 2: Cut yarn. Make another handle the same way.

Attach crocheted handles as for leather handles.

Drawstring Bag

MEASUREMENTS:
Length: approx. 9½ in / 24 cm
Circumference: approx. 18¼ in / 46 cm

MATERIALS:
Yarn: CYCA #3, Marks & Kattens M&K Linen
(100% linen, 136 yd/124 m / 50 g)
Dark Blue 963, 50 g
Blue 957, 50 g
Light Blue 964, 50 g

Crochet Hook: U.S. size D-3 / 3.25 mm;
U.S. size E-4 / 3.5 mm for foundation chain

GAUGE:
19 sc with smaller hook = 4 in / 10 cm.
Adjust hook size to obtain correct gauge if
necessary.

1 pattern repeat = 8 sts

When changing colors, bring new color through
on the last step of the last st of the previous
row. This produces a "complete" color on the
first st of the next row.

Crochet Stitches Used: Chain st (ch), slip st
(sl st), single crochet (sc), double crochet (dc),
crab stitch (see pages 110-117).

( ) Repeat the sequence within parentheses
the number of times specified after the end
parenthesis.

INSTRUCTIONS FOR DRAWSTRING BAG:
With Dark Blue and larger hook, ch 7 and join into
a ring with 1 sl st into 1st ch.
Rnd 1: Change to smaller hook. Work 16 sc
around ring, ending with 1 sl st into 1st ch.
Rnd 2: Ch 1, (1 sc in next sc, 2 sc in next sc) 8
times; end with 1 sl st into 1st ch = 24 sc.
Rnd 3: Ch 1, work 1 sc in each sc around, ending
with 1 sl st into 1st ch = 24 sc.
Rnd 4: Ch 1, (1 sc in each of next 2 sc, 2 sc in
next sc) 8 times, end with 1 sl st into 1st ch =
32 sc.
Rnd 5: Ch 1, work 1 sc in each sc around, ending
with 1 sl st into 1st ch = 32 sc.
Rnd 6: Ch 1, (1 sc in each of next 3 sc, 2 sc in
next sc) 8 times, end with 1 sl st into 1st ch =
40 sc.
Rnd 7: Ch 1, work 1 sc in each sc around, ending
with 1 sl st into 1st ch = 40 sc.
Rnd 8: Ch 1, (1 sc in each of next 4 sc, 2 sc in
next sc) 8 times, end with 1 sl st into 1st ch =
48 sc.
Rnd 9: Ch 1, (1 sc in each of next 5 sc, 2 sc in
next sc) 8 times, end with 1 sl st into 1st ch =
56 sc.
Rnd 10: Ch 1, (1 sc in each of next 6 sc, 2 sc in
next sc) 8 times, end with 1 sl st into 1st ch =
64 sc.
Rnd 11: Ch 1, work 1 sc in each sc around, ending
with 1 sl st into 1st ch = 64 sc.
Rnd 12: Ch 1, (1 sc in each of next 7 sc, 2 sc in
next sc) 8 times, end with 1 sl st into 1st ch =
72 sc.
Rnd 13: Ch 1, work 1 sc in each sc around,
ending with 1 sl st into 1st ch = 72 sc.
Rnd 14: Ch 1, (1 sc in each of next 8 sc, 2 sc in
next sc) 8 times, end with 1 sl st into 1st ch =
80 sc.
Rnd 15: Ch 1, work 1 sc in each sc around,
ending with 1 sl st into 1st ch = 80 sc.
Rnd 16: Ch 1, (1 sc in each of next 9 sc, 2 sc in
next sc) 8 times, end with 1 sl st into 1st ch =
88 sc.
Rnd 17: Ch 1, work 1 sc in each sc around, ending
with 1 sl st into 1st ch = 88 sc.
Rnd 18: Ch 1, (1 sc in each of next 10 sc, 2 sc in
next sc) 8 times, end with 1 sl st into 1st ch =
96 sc.
Rnd 19: Ch 1, work 1 sc through back loop in
each sc around, ending with 1 sl st into 1st ch =
96 sc. This rnd is the transition between the base
and sides of the bag.
Rnd 20: Ch 1, 1 sc in each sc around, ending with
1 sl st into 1st ch.
Rnds 21-25: Work as for Rnd 20, changing to Blue

on last step of last st of Rnd 25; cut Dark Blue.

Rnd 25: With Blue, ch 1, *1 long sc into sc 2 rows below, 1 long sc in sc 3 rows below, 1 long sc in sc 4 rows below, 1 long sc in sc 3 rows below, 1 long sc in sc 2 rows below, 1 sc in each of next 3 sc*; rep from * to * around, ending with 1 sl st into 1st ch.

Rnd 26: Ch 1, 1 sc in each sc around, ending with 1 sl st into 1st ch.

Rnds 27-30: Work as for Rnd 26, changing to Light Blue on final step of last sc on Rnd 30; cut Blue.

Rnd 31: With Light Blue, ch 1, 1 long sc in sc 2 rows below, *(1 sc in next sc) 3 times, 1 long sc in sc 2 rows below, 1 long sc in sc 3 rows below, 1 long sc in sc 4 rows below, 1 long sc in sc 3 rows below, 1 long sc in sc 2 rows below*; rep * to * around, ending with (1 sc in next sc) 3 times, 1 long sc in sc 2 rows below, 1 long sc in sc 3 rows below, 1 long sc in sc 4 rows below, 1 long sc in sc 3 rows below, 1 sl st into 1st ch.

Rnd 32: Ch 1, 1 sc in each sc around, ending with 1 sl st into 1st ch.

Rnds 33-36: Work as for Rnd 32, changing to Dark Blue on last step of last st of Rnd 25; cut Light Blue.

Rnd 37: With Dark Blue, ch 1, *1 long sc into sc 2 rows below, 1 long sc in sc 3 rows below, 1 long sc in sc 4 rows below, 1 long sc in sc 3 rows below, 1 long sc in sc 2 rows below, 1 sc in each of next 3 sc*; rep from * to * around, ending with 1 sl st into 1st ch.

Rnd 38: Ch 1, 1 sc in each sc around, ending with 1 sl st into 1st ch.

Rnds 39-42: Work as for Rnd 38, changing to Blue on final step of last sc on Rnd 42; cut Light Blue.

Rnd 43: With Blue, ch 1, 1 long sc in sc 2 rows below, *(1 sc in next sc) 3 times, 1 long sc in sc 2 rows below, 1 long sc in sc 3 rows below, 1 long sc in sc 4 rows below, 1 long sc in sc 3 rows below, 1 long sc in sc 2 rows below*; rep * to * around, ending with (1 sc in next sc) 3 times, 1 long sc in sc 2 rows below, 1 long sc in sc 3 rows below, 1 long sc in sc 4 rows below, 1 long sc in sc 3 rows below, 1 sl st into 1st ch.

Rnd 44: Ch 1, 1 sc in each sc around, ending with 1 sl st into 1st ch.

Rnds 45-48: Work as for Rnd 44, changing to Light Blue on last step of last st of Rnd 25; cut Blue.

Rnd 49: With Light Blue, ch 1, *1 long sc into sc 2 rows below, 1 long sc in sc 3 rows below, 1 long sc in sc 4 rows below, 1 long sc in sc 3 rows below, 1 long sc in sc 2 rows below, 1 sc in each of next 3 sc*; rep from * to * around, ending with 1 sl st into 1st ch.

Rnd 50: Ch 1, 1 sc in each sc around, ending with 1 sl st into 1st ch.

Rnds 51-71: Work as for Rnd 50.

Rnd 72 (eyelet round): Ch 4, *skip 1 sc, 1 dc in each of next 3 sc, ch 1*; rep from * to * around, ending with skip 1 sc, 1 dc in each of next 2 sc, 1 sl st into top of ch 3.

Rnd 73: Ch 1, *1 sc around ch, 1 sc in each of next 3 dc*; rep from * to * around, ending with 1 sc in ch, 1 sc in each of next 2 dc, 1 sl st into 1st ch.

Rnds 74-78: Work as for Rnd 71, changing to Dark Blue on final step of last st on Rnd 78; cut Light Blue.

Rnd 79: With Dark Blue, ch 1, 1 long sc in sc 2 rows below, *(1 sc in next sc) 3 times, 1 long sc in sc 2 rows below, 1 long sc in sc 3 rows below, 1 long sc in sc 4 rows below, 1 long sc in sc 3 rows below, 1 long sc in sc 2 rows below*; rep * to * around, ending with (1 sc in next sc) 3 times, 1 long sc in sc 2 rows below, 1 long sc in sc 3 rows below, 1 long sc in sc 4 rows below, 1 long sc in sc 3 rows below, 1 sl st into 1st ch.

Rnd 80: Ch 1, 1 sc in each sc around, ending with 1 sl st into 1st ch.

Rnds 81-83: Work as for Rnd 80.

Rnd 84: Ch 1, 1 crab st in each sc around, end with 1 sl st into 1st ch.

FINISHING:
Weave in all ends neatly on WS.

TIE CORDS:
With 6 lengths of doubled yarn, twist two cords 23¾ in / 60 cm long. Measure or count to the center on each side of the bag and thread the cords through eyelet round in from the respective sides; knot at each end.

Soft Scarf

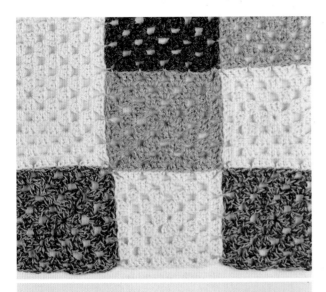

This scarf is composed of three different sizes of squares that are joined as for a quilt. The blocks are crocheted with yarn held double which allows you to have many more "colors" than just the 3 listed in the materials. Combine beige and white, beige and beige, gray and beige, white and gray, gray and gray, white and white and you will have quite a variety of block colors. You can also decide on how many of each size square you want.

MEASUREMENTS:
Approx. 14 x 59 in / 35 x 150 cm

CROCHET

Small square, approx. 1½ x 1½ in / 3.5 x 3.5 cm
Medium square, approx. 2¾ x 2¾ in / 7 x 7 cm
Large square, approx. 5½ x 5½ in / 14 x 14 cm

MATERIALS:
Yarn: CYCA #0, Skaska Belisa Cashmere 1
(100% cashmere, 1054 yd/964 m / 100 g)
Natural White, 100 g
Beige, 100 g
Gray Heather, 100 g
Alternate Yarn: CYCA #0, Artyarns Cashmere 1
(100% cashmere, 510 yd/466 m / 50 g)
Natural White, 100 g
Beige, 100 g
Gray, 100 g

Crochet Hook: U.S. size E-4 / 3.5 mm

GAUGE:
6.5 pattern repeats with yarn held double =
4 in / 10 cm.
Adjust hook size to obtain correct gauge if
necessary.

1 pattern repeat = 4 sts

Crochet Stitches Used: Chain st (ch), slip stitch
(sl st), single crochet (sc), double crochet (dc)
(see pages 110-117).

( ) Repeat the sequence within parentheses
the number of times specified after the end
parenthesis.

INSTRUCTIONS:
The granny squares are made with yarn held
double and sewn together with a single strand of
yarn.

ONE GRANNY SQUARE:
Ch 6 and join into a ring with 1 sl st.

Rnd 1: Ch 6 (= 1 dc + 3 ch), (3 dc around ring, ch
3) 3 times, 2 dc around ring, end rnd with 1 sl st
into top of ch 3 at beg of rnd.
Rnd 2: Sl st to center of 1st ch loop, ch 6 (= 1 dc
+ 3 ch), 3-dc group on same ch loop, *ch 1, (3-dc
gr, ch 3, 3-dc gr) on next ch loop*; rep from * to
* 2 times, ch 1, 2 dc in same ch loop as beg of
rnd with ch 6. End rnd with 1 sl st into top of ch
3 at beg of rnd. The small square ends here.
Rnd 3: Sl st to center of 1st ch loop, ch 6 (= 1 dc
+ 3 ch), 3-dc group on same ch loop, *ch 1, 3
dc on next ch, ch 1,** (3-dc gr, ch 3, 3-dc gr) on
next ch loop; rep from * 2 times and from * to **
1 time, 2 dc in same ch loop as beg of rnd with
ch 6. End rnd with 1 sl st into top of ch 3 at beg
of rnd.
Rnd 4: Sl st to center of 1st ch loop, ch 6 (= 1 dc
+ 3 ch), 3-dc group on same ch loop, *ch 1, (3 dc
on next ch, ch 1) 2 times,** (3-dc gr, ch 3, 3-dc
gr) on next ch loop*; rep from * 2 times and from
* to ** 1 time, 2 dc in same ch loop as beg of
rnd with ch 6. End rnd with 1 sl st into 3rd of beg
ch. The medium square ends here.
Rnd 5: Work as for Rnd 4 but with 1 3-dc gr more
on each side of the square.

Rnd 6: Work as for Rnd 5 but with 1 3-dc gr more on each side of the square.

Rnd 7: Work as for Rnd 6 but with 1 3-dc gr more on each side of the square.

Rnd 8: Work as for Rnd 7 but with 1 3-dc gr more on each side of the square. The large square ends here.

The scarf consists of 36 small squares, 60 medium squares, and 8 large squares. You can decide how many squares of each size you want to combine for your scarf.

FINISHING:

Weave in all ends neatly on WS.
With WS facing, sew the squares together with a single strand of Beige. Place squares 1 and 2 together with RS facing RS. Begin seaming at one corner with 1 sc through the ch loops on each square, *ch 4, skip 1 3-dc gr and then work 1 sl st through both layers*; rep from * to * to the corner and work 1 sc through the ch loops of both squares.

Tip: Join blocks of 4 small size squares which will then be the same size as the medium squares. These can then be joined to the larger squares.

Edging: With yarn held double, begin in one corner with **2 sc, ch 2, 2 sc in corner**; *ch 3, skip 1 3-dc gr, 2 sc around ch*; rep from * to * to next corner; rep ** to ** in each corner and end each side with ch 3 before the corner. Rep ** to ** in each corner. End rnd with 1 sl st into 1st ch.

Unisex Scarf

CROCHET

This scarf has only one pattern row that is repeated throughout. It's the perfect project for a beginner or when you need a "no-brainer."

MEASUREMENTS:
Approx. 13½ x 73 in / 34 x 185 cm

MATERIALS:
Yarn: CYCA #1, Katia Darling (60% Merino wool, 40% polyamide, 207 yd/189 m / 50 g)
Multi-color black-beige, 207, 250 g

Crochet Hook: U.S. size E-4 / 3.5 mm + U.S. size F-5 / 3.75 mm for beg chain

GAUGE:
2 pattern repeats (= 28 sts) with smaller size hook = 4 in / 10 cm.
Adjust hook size to obtain correct gauge if necessary.

1 pattern repeat = 14 sts

Crochet Stitches Used: Chain st (ch), slip stitch (sl st), double crochet (dc) (see pages 110-113).

( ) Repeat the sequence within parentheses the number of times specified after the end parenthesis.

INSTRUCTIONS:
With larger size hook, ch 87.
Row 1: Change to smaller size hook. Beg in 4th ch from hook (= 1st dc), work 1 dc into each of next 5 ch, *skip 2 ch, 1 dc in each of next 6 ch, ch 2, 1 dc in each of next 6 ch*; rep from * to *, skip 2 ch, 1 dc in each of next 6 ch; turn.
Row 2: Ch 4 (= 1st dc), 2 dc in next dc, 1 dc in each of next 3 dc, *skip 2 dc, 1 dc in each of next 5 dc, 1 dc around ch loop, ch 1, 1 dc around same ch loop, 1 dc in each of next 5 dc*; rep from * to * and end with skip 2 dc, 1 dc in each of next 3 dc, 2 dc in next dc, 1 dc in 3rd ch; turn.
Row 3: Work as for Row 2.
Row 4 and all following rows: Work as for Row 2 until scarf is approx. 73 in / 185 cm long or the last ball of yarn is used up.

FINISHING:
Weave in all ends neatly on WS. Lightly steam press scarf.

Fan Pattern Pillow

Back of pillow

MEASUREMENTS:
Approx. 18¾ x 18¾ in / 47.5 x 47.5 cm

MATERIALS:
Yarn: CYCA #4, Lion Brand Fishermen's wool (100% wool, 465 yd/425 m / 8 oz/227 g) Oatmeal 123, 350 g

Alternate Yarn: CYCA #5, Rauma/PT Puno Alpaca (68% alpaca, 22% nylon, 10% Merino wool, 120 yd/110 m / 50 g

Notions: Pillow form 20 x 20 in / 50 x 50 cm

Crochet Hook: U.S. size H-8 / 5 mm and U.S. size J-9 / 5.5 mm for back

GAUGE:
2½ pattern repeats (15 sts) with smaller size hook = 4 in / 10 cm.
Adjust hook size to obtain correct gauge if necessary.

1 pattern repeat = 6 sts

Crochet Stitches Used: Chain st (ch), slip stitch (sl st), single crochet (sc), extended double crochet (edc), crab st (see pages 110-117).

( ) Repeat the sequence within parentheses the number of times specified after the end parenthesis.

INSTRUCTIONS:
FRONT:
With larger size hook, ch 74.
Row 1 (WS): Work 1 sc in 2nd ch from hook and then 1 sc in each ch across = 73 sc; turn.
Row 2 (RS): Ch 1,*1 sc in next sc, skip 2 sc, 5 edc in next sc (= 1 fan), skip 2 sc*; rep from * to * across, ending with 1 sc in last sc; turn.
Row 3: Ch 4 (= 1 edc), 2 edc in same sc (= ½ fan), *skip 2 edc, 1 sc in next edc (= top of fan), skip 2 edc, 1 fan in next sc*; rep from * to * across, ending with skip 2 edc, 1 sc in next edc, skip 2 edc, 3 edc in sc (= ½ fan); turn.
Row 4: Ch 1, 1 sc in edc, skip 2 edc, *1 fan in sc, skip 2 edc, 1 sc in next edc, skip 2 edc*; rep from * to * across, ending with 1 fan in sc, skip 2 edc, 1 sc in top of ch 4; turn.
Row 5: Work as for Row 3.
Row 6: Work as for Row 4.
Row 7: Work as for Row 3.
Row 8: Work as for Row 4.
Continue, repeating Rows 3-4, until the piece is approx. 18¾ in / 47.5 cm long. End with 1 row of 1 sc in each sc and edc across. Cut yarn.

BACK:
With larger size hook, ch 67.
Row 1 (RS): Change to smaller hook and work 1 edc in the 5th ch from hook. Continue with 1 edc in each ch across = 63 edc; turn.
Row 2: Ch 4, 1 edc in back loop of each edc across = 63 edc; turn.
Row 3: Ch 4, 1 edc in back loop of each edc across, ending with 1 edc in top of ch 4 = 63 edc; turn.
Repeat Row 3 until piece is same length as the pillow front. End with 1 row sc and then cut yarn.

FINISHING (Read through *before* beginning work):
Weave in all ends neatly on WS. Place the back and front pieces with WS facing WS and pin together, stretching back to same length as front. Crochet the pieces together with sc, making sure the edges do not ruffle or pull in as you work around. Hold the pillow cover with the front facing you. Begin at the lower edge at one side, work up, across the top, and down the other side. Do not work across bottom.
NOTE: At each corner, work 3 sc in corner st so the edging doesn't draw in. After working sc, work 1 crab st in each sc up side, across top, and down opposite side. Cut yarn and weave in ends. Insert the pillow form, join the bottom of the pillow cover with slip st, and work back with 1 crab st in each sl st. Cut yarn and weave in ends to inside.

Crossed Stitch Pillow

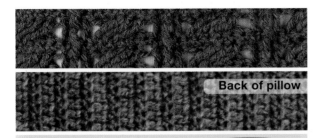

Back of pillow

CROCHET

MEASUREMENTS:
Approx. 18¾ x 18¾ in / 47.5 x 47.5 cm

MATERIALS:
Yarn: CYCA #4, Lion Brand Fishermen's wool
(100% wool, 465 yd/425 m / 8 oz/227 g)
Brown Heather 125, 400 g
Alternate Yarn: CYCA #5, Rauma/PT Puno
Alpaca (68% alpaca, 22% nylon, 10% Merino
wool, 120 yd/110 m / 50 g)

Notions: Pillow form 20 x 20 in / 50 x 50 cm

Crochet Hook: U.S. size H-8 / 5 mm +
U.S. size J-9 / 5.5 mm for back

GAUGE:
2 pattern repeats (18 sts) with smaller size hook
= 4½ in / 11.5 cm.
Adjust hook size to obtain correct gauge if
necessary.

1 pattern repeat = 9 sts

Crochet Stitches Used: Chain st (ch), slip st
(sl st), single crochet (sc), half double crochet
(hdc), double crochet (dc), back post double
crochet (BPdc), front post treble crochet (FPtr),
triple treble crochet (tr tr) (see pages 110-117).

( ) Repeat the sequence within parentheses
the number of times specified after the end
parenthesis.

INSTRUCTIONS:
FRONT:
With smaller size hook, ch 79.
Row 1 (WS): Work 1 hdc in 3rd ch from hook, and
then 1 hdc in each ch across = 77 hdc; turn.
Row 2 (RS): Ch 3 (= 1st dc), *1 dc in hdc, 1 FPtr
around hdc, 1 dc in hdc, skip 3 hdc, 1 FPtr tr in
next hdc, 1 tr tr in each of next 2 hdc, go back to
the first hdc of the 3 skipped, 1 tr tr in hdc (this
and the next 2 tr tr are worked behind the 3 tr tr

which have already been worked), 1 tr tr in each
of next 2 hdc*; rep * to * across, endiing with 1
dc in hdc, 1 FPtr around hdc, 1 dc in each of next
2 hdc; turn.
Row 3: Ch 1, 1 sc in dc, *1 sc in dc, 1 BPdc
around 1 FPtr, 1 sc in dc, (1 sc in tr tr) 6 times*;
rep * to *across, ending with 1 dc in sc, 1 BPdc
around 1 FPtr, 1 dc in sc, 1 dc in top of ch 3;
turn.
Row 4: Ch 3 (= 1st dc), *1 dc in sc, 1 FPtr around
1 BPdc, 1 dc in sc, skip 3 sc, 1 tr tr in next sc,
(1 tr tr in next sc) 2 times, go back to the first sc
of the 3 skipped, 1 tr tr in sc (this and the next
2 tr tr are worked behind the 3 tr tr which have
already been worked), 1 tr tr in each of next 2
sc*; rep * to * across, ending with 1 dc in sc, 1
FPtr around 1 BPdc, 1 dc in each of next 2 sc;
turn.
Row 5: Work as for Row 3.
Row 6: Work as for Row 4.
Row 7: Work as for Row 3.
Row 8: Work as for Row 4.
Continue repeating Rows 3-4 until the front measures approx. 18¾ in / 47.5 cm. End with Row 3
and then work 1 row of 1 sc in each st across;
cut yarn.

BACK:
With larger size hook, ch 67.
Row 1 (RS): Change to smaller hook and work 1
sc in the 2nd ch from hook. Continue with 1 sc in
each ch across = 63 sc; turn.
Row 2: Ch 3 (= 1st dc), 1 dc in back loop of each
sc across = 63 dc; turn.
Row 3: Ch 1, 1 sc in each dc across = 63 sc; turn.
Repeat Rows 2-3 until piece is same length as
the pillow front. End with Row 3 and then cut
yarn.

FINISHING (Read through *before* beginning work):
Weave in all ends neatly on WS. Place the back
and front pieces with WS facing WS and pin
together, stretching back to same length as front.
Crochet the pieces together with sc, making sure
the edges do not ruffle or pull in as you work
around. Hold the pillow cover with the front facing you. Begin at the lower edge at one side,
work up, across the top, and down the other
side. Do not work across bottom.
NOTE: At each corner, work 3 sc in corner st so
the edging doesn't draw in. Cut yarn and weave
in ends.
Insert the pillow form; join the bottom of the
pillow cover with slip st. Cut yarn and weave in
ends to inside.

Pillow with Bobbles

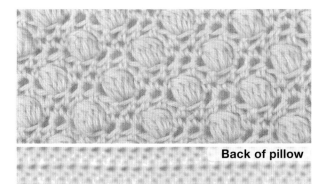

Back of pillow

CROCHET

MEASUREMENTS:
Approx. 18¾ x 11 in / 47.5 x 28 cm

MATERIALS:
Yarn: CYCA #4, Lion Brand Fishermen's wool
(100% wool, 465 yd/425 m / 8 oz/227 g)
Natural 098, 300 g
Alternate Yarn: CYCA #5, Rauma/PT Puno
Alpaca (68% alpaca, 22% nylon, 10% Merino
wool, 120 yd/110 m / 50 g)

Notions: Pillow form 20 x 12 in / 50 x 30 cm

Crochet Hook: U.S. size H-8 / 5 mm +
U.S. size J-9 / 5.5 mm for back

GAUGE:
13 pattern sts with smaller size hook =
4 in / 10 cm.
Adjust hook size to obtain correct gauge if
necessary.

1 pattern repeat = 4 sts

Crochet Stitches Used: Chain st (ch), slip stitch
(sl st), single crochet (sc), half double crochet
(hdc), bobble, crab st (see pages 110-117).

( ) Repeat the sequence within parentheses
the number of times specified after the end
parenthesis.

INSTRUCTIONS:
FRONT:
With larger size hook, ch 64.
Row 1 (RS): Change to smaller hook and work 1

sc in 2nd ch from hook and then 1 sc in each ch
across = 63 sc; turn.
Row 2 (WS): Ch 2, *1 hdc in each sc across = 63
hdc; turn.
Row 3: Ch 1, *(1 sc in hdc) 3 times, 1 bobble in
hdc (= 5 dc in same st, decreased to 1 st—see
how to crochet bobbles on page 116)*; rep from
* to * across, ending with (1 sc in hdc) 3 times;
turn.
Row 4: Ch 2, 1 hdc in each sc and bobble across;
turn.
Row 5: Ch 1, 1 sc in hdc, *1 bobble in hdc, (1 sc
in hdc) 3 times*; rep from * to * across, ending
with 1 bobble in hdc, 1 sc in hdc; turn.
Row 6: Work as for Row 4.
Row 7: Work as for Row 3.
Row 8: Work as for Row 4.
Row 9: Work as for Row 5.
Continue, repeating Rows 6-9, until the piece is
approx. 11 in / 28 cm long. End with 1 bobble
row (either Row 3 or 5) and then work Row 4 fol-
lowed by a row with 1 sc in each hdc across. Cut
yarn.

BACK:
With larger size hook, ch 67.
Row 1 (RS): Change to smaller hook. Work 1 sc in
2nd ch from hook and then 1 sc in each ch across
= 63 sc; turn.
Row 2 (WS): Ch 2, 1 hdc in each sc across = 63
hdc; turn.
Row 3: Ch 1, 1 sc in each hdc across = 63 hdc;
turn.
Repeat Rows 2-3 until piece is same length as
the pillow front. End with Row 3 and then cut
yarn.

FINISHING (Read through *before* beginning work):
Weave in all ends neatly on WS. Place the back
and front pieces with WS facing WS and pin
together, stretching back to same length as front.
Crochet the pieces together with sc, making sure
the edges do not ruffle or pull in as you work
around. Hold the pillow cover with the front facing you. Begin at the lower edge at one side,
work up, across the top, and down the other
side. Do not work across bottom.
NOTE: At each corner, work 3 sc in corner st so
the edging doesn't draw in. After working sc,
work 1 crab st in each sc up side, across top, and
down opposite side. Cut yarn and weave in ends.
Insert the pillow form, join the bottom of the pillow cover with slip st, and work back with 1 crab
st in each sl st. Cut yarn and weave in ends to
inside.

Fan Pattern Scarf

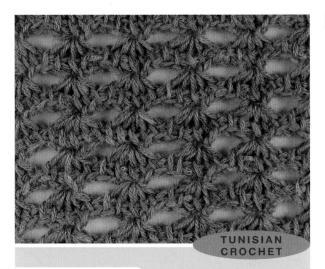

TUNISIAN CROCHET

MEASUREMENTS:
Approx. 11½ x 63 in / 29 x 160 cm

MATERIALS:
Yarn: CYCA #1, Du Store Alpakka Dreamline Sky (70% baby alpaca, 30% silk, 128 yd/117 m / 25 g) / Sky Blue DL303, 125 g

CYCA #0, Du Store Alpakka Dreamline Soul (68% baby alpaca, 32% nylon, 195 yd/178 m / 25 g) / Heather Blue/Rose tones DL212, 100 g

Tunisian Crochet Hook: U.S. size L-11 / 8 mm for scarf
Crochet Hook: U.S. size K-10½ / 6.5 mm for beginning chain and finishing

GAUGE:
18 vertical sts or 3.5 pattern repeats with Tunisian crochet hook and 1 strand of each yarn held together = 4 in / 10 cm.
Adjust hook size to obtain correct gauge if necessary.

1 pattern repeat = 5 sts

NOTE: Hold one strand of each yarn together throughout.

Crochet Stitches Used: Vertical stitches, fan (see step-by-step instructions for vertical sts on page 122 and for fans on page 126).

INSTRUCTIONS:
With crochet hook U.S. size K-10½ / 6.5 mm and 1 strand of each yarn held together, ch 54 sts.
Row 1, forward: Change to Tunisian crochet hook U.S. size L-11 / 8 mm. Beginning in the 2nd ch from hook, pick up 53 vertical sts in the top loop of each ch = 54 loops.
Row 1, return: Bind off the sts as follows: yarn around hook and through the 1st loop on hook, *yarn around hook and through 2 loops*; rep from * to * across.
Row 2, forward: 1 edge st, pick up *1 vertical st*; rep from * to * across, ending with 1 edge st = 54 loops on hook.
Row 2, return: Bind off all sts.
Row 3, forward: 1 edge st, pick up *1 vertical st*; rep from * to * across, ending with 1 edge st = 54 loops on hook.
Row 3, return: Bind off as follows: yarn around hook and through 1 st, yarn around hook and through 2 sts on hook, ch 2, *yarn around hook and through 6 loops on hook, yarn around hook and through 1 loop to "lock" the fan (= 1 fan), ch 4*; rep from * to * across, ending with bind off 1 fan, ch 2, bind off 1 vertical st, 1 edge st = 54 sts on hook.
Row 4, forward: 1 edge st, pick up 1 vertical st, pick up (1 vertical st in ch) 2 times, *pick up 1 vertical st in top of fan, pick up (1 vertical st in ch) 4 times*; rep from * to * across, ending with pick up 1 vertical st in top of fan, pick up (1 vertical st in ch) 2 times, 1 vertical st, and 1 edge st = 54 sts.
Row 4, return: Bind off all sts.
Row 5, forward and return: Work as for Row 3, forward and return.
Row 6, forward and return: Work as for Row 4, forward and return.
Repeat Rows 3, forward and return, and 4, forward and return, until scarf is 59 in / 150 cm long or desired length. End with Row 2, forward and return.
Edging: Use the regular crochet hook to work 1 sl st into each vertical st across, ending with 1 sl st into edge st.

FINISHING:
Weave in all ends neatly on WS. Dampen scarf and lightly block to finished size.

Cashmere Scarf

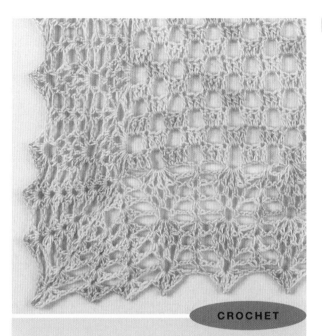

CROCHET

MEASUREMENTS:
Approx. 11¾ x 90½ in / 30 x 230 cm

MATERIALS:
Yarn: CYCA #0, Artyarns Cashmere 1 (100% cashmere, 510 yd/466 m / 50 g) / Beige 167, 250 g

Crochet Hook: U.S. size D-3 / 3.25 mm for scarf; U.S. size E-4 / 3.5 mm for foundation chain

GAUGE:
5 pattern repeats of inner motif with 6 sts each (= 30 sts) with yarn held double and smaller hook = 4 in / 10 cm.
Adjust hook size to obtain correct gauge if necessary.

Inner Motif: 1 pattern repeat = 6 sts

Crochet Stitches Used: Chain st (ch), slip stitch (sl st), single crochet (sc), double crochet (dc) (see pages 110-117).

NOTE: Hold two strands of yarn together throughout.

INSTRUCTIONS:
INNER MOTIF:
With larger hook and yarn held doubled, ch 54.
Row 1: Change to smaller hook and begin with 1 dc in the 4th ch from hook, then work 1 dc in each of the next 3 ch, *ch 2, skip 2 ch, 1 dc in each of next 4 ch*; rep from * to * across; turn.
Row 2: Ch 5 (= 1st dc + 2 ch), skip 2 dc, *1 dc in next dc, 2 dc around ch loop, 1 dc in next dc, ch 2, skip 2 dc*; rep from * to * across, ending with 1 dc in 3rd ch; turn.
Row 3: Ch 3 (= 1st dc), *2 dc around ch loop, 1 dc in next dc, ch 2, skip 2 dc, 1 dc in next dc*; rep from * to * across, ending with 2 dc around ch loop; 1 dc in top of tc; turn.
Row 4: Work as for Row 2.
Row 5: Work as for Row 3.
Repeat Rows 2 and 3 until piece is approx. 63 in / 160 cm long and there are an odd number of open "blocks" along the edge. The inner motif ends with Row 3. Cut yarn.

Edging: Work with smaller size hook and yarn held doubled.
Rnd 1: Begin at a corner on one short side (the short side is worked first): Attach yarn with 1 sl st into the corner.
1st short side: 1 sc in the corner, ch 3, skip 4 dc (= 1 complete block), 1 dc around ch loop, ch 1, 1 dc around the same ch loop, ch 1, 1 dc around the same ch loop, ch 1, 1 dc round the same ch loop, ch 1, 1 dc around same ch loop (= 1 fan), *ch 2, skip 1 complete block, 1 sc around ch loop, ch 2, skip 1 complete block, 1 fan around next ch loop*; rep from * to * to the corner, ending with ch 3, 1 sc in corner.
1st long side: Ch 3, *1 fan around next ch loop, ch 2, skip 1 complete block, 1 sc around next ch loop, ch 2, skip 1 complete block*; rep from * to * across, ending long side with ch 2, 1 fan around ch loop, ch 3, skip 1 complete block, 1 sc in corner.
Work the 2nd short side as for the first and the 2nd long side as for 1st long side. End with 1 sl st in the sc in corner.
Rnd 2:
1st corner: Ch 4 (= 1st dc + ch 1), 1 dc in sc, ch 2,

49

1 dc in same sc, ch 1, 1 dc in same sc.

1st short side: *Ch 1, skip 2 ch and 1 dc, (1 sc in ch, ch 3, skip 1 dc) 3 times, 1 sc in ch, ch 1, skip 1 dc and 2 ch, 1 dc in sc, ch 1, 1 dc in same sc*; rep from * to * across short side, ending with ch 1, skip 2 ch and 1 dc, (1 sc in ch, ch 3, skip 1 dc) 3 times, 1 sc in ch, ch 1, skip 1 dc and 3 ch.

2nd corner: 1 dc in sc, ch 1, 1 dc in same sc, ch 2, 1 dc in same sc, ch 1, 1 dc in same sc.

1st long side: Work as for 1st short side.

3rd corner: Work as for 2nd corner.

2nd short side: Work as for 1st short side.

2nd long side: Work as for 1st short side. End rnd with 1 sl st into 3rd ch at beg of rnd.

Rnd 3:

1st corner: 1 dc around ch, ch 1, 2 dc around same ch, ch 1, 1 dc around ch loop, ch 1, 1 dc around same ch loop, ch 1, 2 dc around ch, ch 1, 2 dc around same ch.

1st short side: *Ch 2, skip 1 dc, 1 ch and 1 sc, (1 sc around ch loop, ch 3, skip 1 sc) 2 times, 1 sc around ch loop, ch 2, skip 1 sc, 1 ch and 1 dc, 1 dc around ch, ch 1, 1 dc around same ch*; rep from * to * across short side, ending with ch 2, skip 1 dc, 1 ch and 1 sc, (1 sc around ch loop, ch 3, skip 1 sc) 2 times, 1 sc around ch loop, ch 2, skip 1 sc and 1 dc.

2nd corner: 2 dc around ch, ch 1, 2 dc around same ch, ch 1, 1 dc around ch loop, ch 1, 1 dc around same ch loop, ch 1, 2 dc around ch, ch 1, 2 dc around same ch.

1st long side: Work as for 1st short side.

3rd corner: Work as for 2nd corner.

2nd short side: Work as for 1st short side.

4th corner: Work as for 2nd corner.

2nd long side: Work as for 1st short side. End rnd with 1 sl st into 3rd ch at beg of rnd.

Rnd 4:

1st corner: 1 sl st into dc, 1 sl st around ch, ch 3 (= 1st dc), 1 dc around same ch, ch 1, 2 dc around same ch, ch 2, skip 2 dc, 1 ch and 1 dc, 2 dc around ch, ch 1, 2 dc around same ch, skip 1 dc, 1 ch and 2 dc, ch 2, 2 dc around ch, ch 1, 2 dc around same ch,

1st short side: Ch 3, skip 2 dc, 1 ch and 1 sc, *1 sc around ch loop, ch 3, 1 sc around next ch loop, ch 3, skip 1 sc, 2 ch and 2 dc, 1 dc around ch, ch 1, 1 dc around same ch, ch 3, skip 1 dc, 2 ch and 1 sc*; rep from * to * across short side, ending with 1 sc around next ch loop, ch 3, skip 1 sc, 2 ch and 1 dc.

2nd corner: 2 dc around ch, ch 1, 2 dc around same ch, ch 2, skip 2 dc, 1 ch and 1 dc, 2 dc around ch, ch 1, 2 dc around same ch, skip 1 dc, 1 ch and 2 dc, ch 2, 2 dc around ch, ch 1, 2 dc

around same ch.

1st long side: Work as for 1st short side.

3rd corner: Work as for 2nd corner.

2nd short side: Work as for 1st short side.

4th corner: Work as for 2nd corner.

2nd long side: Work as for 1st short side. End rnd with 1 sl st into 3rd ch at beg of rnd.

Rnd 5:

1st corner: 1 sl st into dc, 1 sl st around ch, ch 3 (= 1st dc), 1 dc around same ch, ch 1, 2 dc around same ch, ch 1, skip 2 dc, 1 dc around ch loop, ch 1, 1 dc around same ch loop, skip 2 dc, ch 1, 2 dc around ch, ch 1, 2 dc around same ch, skip 2 dc, ch 1, 1 dc around ch loop, ch 1, 1 dc around same ch loop, skip 2 dc, ch 1, 2 dc around ch, ch 1, 2 dc around same loop, skip 2 dc, 3 ch and 1 sc, ch 2.

1st short side: *1 fan around ch loop, ch 2, skip 1 sc, 3 ch and 1 dc, 1 sc around ch, skip 1 dc, 3 ch and 1 sc, ch 2*; rep from * to * across, ending with 1 fan around ch loop, ch 2, skip 1 sc, 3 ch and 2 dc.

2nd corner: 2 dc around ch, ch 1, 2 dc around same ch, ch 1, skip 2 dc, 1 dc around ch loop, ch 1, 1 dc around same ch loop, skip 2 dc, ch 1, 2 dc around ch, ch 1, 2 dc around same ch, skip 2 dc, ch 1, 1 dc around ch loop, ch 1, 1 dc around same ch loop, skip 2 dc, ch 1, 2 dc around ch, ch 1, 2 dc around same ch, skip 2 dc, 3 ch and 1 sc, ch 2.

1st long side: Work as for 1st short side.

3rd corner: Work as for 2nd corner.

2nd short side: Work as for 1st short side.

4th corner: Work as for 2nd corner.

2nd long side: Work as for 1st short side. End rnd with ch 2, 1 sl st into 3rd ch at beg of rnd.

Rnd 6:

1st corner: 1 sl st into dc, 1 sl st around ch, ch 3 (= 1st dc), 1 dc around same ch, ch 1, 2 dc around same ch, ch 1, skip 2 dc, 1 ch and 1 dc, 2 dc around ch, ch 1, 2 dc around same ch, skip 1 dc, 1 ch and 2 dc, ch 1, 2 dc around ch, ch 1, 2 dc around same ch, skip 2 dc, 1 ch and 1 dc, ch 1, 2 dc around ch, ch 1, 2 dc around same ch, skip 1 dc, 1 ch and 2 dc, ch 1, 2 dc around ch, ch 1, 2 dc around same ch, skip 2 dc, 2 ch and 1 dc.

1st short side: *Ch 2, (1 sc around ch, ch 3, skip 1 dc) 3 times, 1 sc around ch, ch 1, skip 1 dc and 2 ch, 1 dc in sc, ch 1, 1 dc in same sc, ch 1, skip 2 ch and 1 dc*; rep from * to * along short side, ending with ch 1, skip 2 ch and 1 dc, (1 sc around ch, ch 3, skip 1 dc) 3 times, 1 sc around ch, ch 1, skip 1 dc, 2 ch, and 2 dc.

2nd corner: 2 dc around ch, ch 1, 2 dc around same ch, ch 1, skip 2 dc, 1 ch and 1 dc, 2 dc around ch, ch 1, 2 dc around same ch, skip 2 dc, 1 ch and 1 dc, ch 1, 2 dc around ch, ch 1, 2 dc around same ch, skip 1 dc, 1 ch and 2 dc, ch 1, 2 dc around ch, ch 1, 2 dc around same ch, skip 2 dc, ch 1, 2 dc around ch, ch 1, 2 dc around same ch, skip 2 dc, 2 ch and 1 dc, 1 sc, ch 2.

1st long side: Work as for 1st short side.

3rd corner: Work as for 2nd corner.

2nd short side: Work as for 1st short side.

4th corner: Work as for 2nd corner.

2nd long side: Work as for 1st short side.

End rnd with 1 sl st into 3rd ch at beg of rnd.

Rnd 7:

1st corner: 1 sl st into dc, 1 sl st around ch, ch 3 (= 1st dc), 1 dc around same ch, ch 1, 2 dc around same ch, ch 1, skip 2 dc, 1 ch and 2 dc, 2 dc around ch, ch 1, 2 dc around same ch, skip 2 dc, 1 ch and 2 dc, ch 1, 3 dc around ch, ch 1, 3 dc around same ch, skip 2 dc, 1 ch and 2 dc, ch 1, 2 dc around ch, ch 1, 2 dc around same ch, skip 2 dc, 1 ch and 2 dc, ch 1, 2 dc around ch, ch 1, 2 dc around same ch.

1st short side: Ch 2, skip 2 dc, 1 ch, and 1 sc, *(1 sc around ch loop, ch 3, skip 1 sc) 2 times, 1 sc around ch loop, ch 2, skip 1 sc, 1 ch and 1 dc, 1 dc around ch, ch 1, 1 dc around same ch, ch 2, skip 1 dc, ch 1, 1 sc*; rep from * to * along short side, ending with (1 sc around ch loop, ch 3, skip 1 sc) 2 times,1 sc around ch loop, ch 2, skip 1 sc, 1 ch and 2 dc.

2nd corner: 2 dc around ch, ch 1, 2 dc around same ch, ch 1, skip 2 dc, 1 ch and 2 dc, 2 dc around ch, ch 1, 2 dc around same ch, skip 2 dc, 1 ch and 2 dc, ch 1, 3 dc around ch, ch 1, 3 dc around same ch, skip 2 dc, 1 ch and 2 dc, ch 1, 2 dc around ch, ch 1, 2 dc around same ch, skip 2 dc, 1 ch and 2 dc, ch 1, 2 dc around ch, ch 1, 2 dc around same ch.

1st long side: Work as for 1st short side.

3rd corner: Work as for 2nd corner.

2nd short side: Work as for 1st short side.

4th corner: Work as for 2nd corner.

2nd long side: Work as for 1st short side.

End rnd with 1 sl st into 3rd ch at beg of rnd.

Rnd 8:

1st corner: 1 sl st into dc, 1 sl st around ch, ch 3 (= 1st dc), 1 dc around same ch, ch 1, 2 dc around same ch, ch 1, skip 2 dc, 1 ch and 2 dc, 2 dc around ch, ch 1, 2 dc around same ch, skip 2 dc, 1 ch and 3 dc, ch 2, 3 dc around ch, ch 1, 3 dc around same ch, skip 2 dc, 1 ch, and 3 dc, ch 2, 3 dc around ch, ch 1, 3 dc around same ch, skip 3 dc, 2 ch and 2 dc, ch 1, 2 dc around ch, ch 1, 2 dc around same ch, skip 2 dc, 1 ch and 2 dc, ch 1, 2 dc around ch, ch 1, 2 dc around same ch.

1st short side: Ch 3, skip 2 dc, 1 ch and 1 sc, * 1 sc around ch loop, ch 3, 1 sc around next ch loop, skip 1 sc, 2 ch and 1 dc, 1 dc around ch, ch 1, 1 dc around same ch, ch 3, skip 1 dc, ch 2, 1 sc*; rep from * to * along short side, ending with 1 sc around ch loop, ch 3, skip 1 sc, 2 ch and 1 dc.

2nd corner: 2 dc around ch, ch 1, 2 dc around same ch, ch 1, skip 2 dc, 1 ch and 2 dc, 2 dc around ch, ch 1, 2 dc around same ch, skip 2 dc, 1 ch and 3 dc, ch 2, 3 dc around ch, ch 1, 3 dc around same ch, skip 3 dc, 1 ch and 2 dc, ch 2, 2 dc around ch, ch 1, 2 dc around same ch, skip 2 dc, 1 ch and 2 dc, ch 1, 2 dc around ch, ch 1, 2 dc around same ch.

1st long side: Work as for 1st short side.

3rd corner: Work as for 2nd corner.

2nd short side: Work as for 1st short side.

4th corner: Work as for 2nd corner.

2nd long side: Work as for 1st short side.

End rnd with 1 sl st into 3rd ch at beg of rnd.

Rnd 9:

1st corner: 1 sl st into dc, 1 sl st around ch, ch 4 (= 1st dc + ch 1), (1 dc around same ch, ch 1) 3 times, ch 1, skip 2 dc, 1 ch and 2 dc, (1 dc around same ch, ch 1) 4 times, ch 2, skip 2 dc, 1 ch and 3 dc, (1 dc in same ch, ch 1) 6 times, ch 2, skip 3 dc, 2 ch and 2 dc, (1 dc around same ch, ch 1) 4 times, ch 1, skip 2 dc, 1 ch and 2 dc, (1 dc around same ch, ch 1) 4 times, ch 1.

1st short side: *1 fan around ch loop, ch 1, skip 1 sc, 3 ch and 1 dc, 1 sc around ch, skip 1 dc, 3 ch and 1 sc, ch 1*; rep from * to * across, ending with 1 fan around ch loop, ch 1, skip 1 sc, 3 ch and 2 dc.

2nd corner: (1 dc around same ch, ch 1) 4 times, ch 1, skip 2 dc, 1 ch and 2 dc, (1 dc around same ch, ch 1) 4 times, ch 2, skip 2 dc, 1 ch and 3 dc, (1 dc around same ch, ch 1) 6 times, ch 2, skip 3 dc, 2 ch and 2 dc, (1 dc around same ch, ch 1) 4 times, ch 1, skip 2 dc, 1 ch, and 2 dc, (1 dc around same ch, ch 1) 4 times, ch 1.

1st long side: Work as for 1st short side.

3rd corner: Work as for 2nd corner.

2nd short side: Work as for 1st short side.

4th corner: Work as for 2nd corner.

2nd long side: Work as for 1st short side.

End rnd with ch 1, 1 sl st into 3rd ch at beg of rnd.

FINISHING:

Weave in all yarn ends neatly on WS. Pin out scarf to finished measurements. Dampen and leave until completely dry.

Romantic Shawl

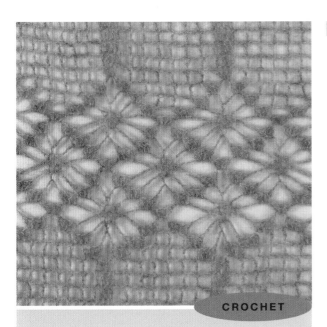

CROCHET

MEASUREMENTS:
Tip to back neck: approx. 35½ in / 90 cm
Wingspan: approx. 90½ in / 230 cm

MATERIALS:
Yarn: CYCA #0, Filatura di Crosa, Superior
(70% cashmere, 25% silk, 5% Merino wool, 330
yd/302 m / 25 g) / Beige 60, 100 g

Crochet Hook: U.S. size D-3 / 3.25 mm

GAUGE:
9 blocks of filet crochet = 4 in / 10 cm.
Adjust hook size to obtain correct gauge if
necessary.

Crochet Stitches Used: Chain st (ch), slip stitch
(sl st), single crochet (sc), double crochet (dc),
extended double crochet (edc), treble crochet
(tr) (see pages 110-117).

( ) Repeat the sequence within parentheses
the number of times specified after the end
parenthesis.

NOTE: Weave in ends along the back loops of
stitches on WS (see page 114).

INSTRUCTIONS:
Row 1: Ch 8, work 4 dc into 1st ch, ch 2, 1 edc in
same (1st) ch; turn.
Row 2: Ch 6, 4 dc around ch loop, ch 4, skip 4
dc, 4 dc around ch loop, ch 2, 1 edc on same ch
loop; turn.
Row 3: Ch 6, 4 dc around ch loop, ch 4, skip 4 dc,
1 sc around ch loop, ch 4, skip 4 dc, 4 dc around
ch loop, ch 2, 1 edc around same ch loop; turn.
Row 4: Ch 6, 4 dc around ch loop, ch 4, skip 4 dc,
1 sc around ch loop, 1 sc in sc, 1 sc around ch
loop, ch 4, skip 4 dc, 4 dc around ch loop, ch 2, 1
edc around same ch loop; turn.
Row 5: Ch 6, 4 dc around ch loop, ch 4, skip 4 dc,
1 sc around ch loop, 1 sc in each of next 3 sc, 1
sc around ch loop, ch 4, skip 4 dc, 4 dc around ch
loop, ch 2, 1 edc around same ch loop; turn.
Row 6: Ch 6, 4 dc around next ch loop, ch 4, skip
4 dc, 4 dc around ch loop, ch 4, 1 sc in each of
the 3 center sc, ch 4, 4 dc around ch loop, skip 4
dc, 4 dc around ch loop, ch 2, 1 edc around same
ch loop; turn.
Row 7: Ch 6, 4 dc around next ch loop, ch 4, skip
4 dc, 1 sc around ch loop, ch 4, skip 4 dc, 4 dc
around ch loop, ch 4, 1 sc in the center of the 3
sc, ch 4, 4 dc around next ch loop, skip 4 dc, ch
4, 1 sc around next ch loop, ch 4, skip 4 dc, 4 dc
around ch loop, ch 2, 1 edc around same ch loop;
turn.
Row 8: Ch 6, 4 dc around next ch loop, ch 4, skip
4 dc, 1 sc around ch loop, 1 sc in sc, 1 sc around
next ch loop, ch 4, skip 4 dc, 4 dc around next ch
loop, ch 2, 4 dc around ch loop, ch 4, skip 4 dc, 1
sc around ch loop, 1 sc in sc, 1 sc around next ch
loop, ch 4, skip 4 dc, 4 dc around ch loop, ch 2, 1
edc around same ch loop; turn.
Row 9: Ch 6, 4 dc around next ch loop, ch 4, skip
4 dc, 1 sc around next ch loop, 1 sc in each of
the 3 sc, 1 sc around next ch loop, ch 4, 4 dc
around the ch-2 loop, ch 4, 1 sc around next ch
loop, 1 sc in each of the 3 sc, 1 sc around next
ch loop, ch 4, skip 4 dc, 4 dc around ch loop, ch
2, 1 edc around same ch loop; turn.
Row 10: Ch 6, 4 dc around next ch loop, *ch 4,
skip 4 dc, 4 dc around ch loop, ch 4, 1 sc in each
of the 3 center sc, ch 4, 4 dc around loop*; rep

from * to * across, ending with ch 4, skip 4 dc, 4 dc around ch loop, ch 2, 1 edc on same ch loop; turn.

Row 11: Ch 6, 4 dc around ch loop, ch 4, skip 4 dc, 1 sc around ch loop, ch 4, skip 4 dc, 4 dc around ch loop, ch 4, 1 sc in the center of the 3 sc, ch 4, 4 dc around next ch loop, ch 4, skip 4 dc, 1 sc around next ch loop, ch 4, skip 4 dc, 4 dc around ch loop, ch 4, 1 sc in the center of the 3 sc, ch 4, 4 dc around next ch loop, ch 4, skip 4 dc, 1 sc around next ch loop, ch 4, skip 4 dc, 4 dc around ch loop, ch 2, 1 edc around same ch loop; turn.

Row 12: Ch 6, *4 dc around ch loop, ch 4, skip 4 dc, 1 sc around ch loop, 1 sc in sc, 1 sc around next ch loop, ch 4, skip 4 dc, 4 dc around next ch loop, ch 2*; rep from * to * across, ending with 1 edc on same ch loop; turn.

Row 13: Ch 6, 4 dc around ch loop, *ch 4, skip 4 dc, 1 sc around next ch loop, 1 sc in each of the 3 sc, 1 sc around next ch loop, ch 4, skip 4 dc, 4 dc around ch loop*; rep from * to * across, ending with ch 2, 1 edc around same ch loop; turn.

Row 14: Ch 6, 4 dc around next ch loop, *ch 4, skip 4 dc, 4 dc around ch loop, ch 4, 1 sc in each of the 3 center sc, ch 4, 4 dc around ch loop*; rep from * to * across, ending with ch 4, skip 4 dc, 4 dc around ch loop, ch 2, 1 edc in same ch loop; turn.

Row 15: Ch 6, *4 dc around ch loop, ch 4, skip 4 dc, 1 sc around ch loop, ch 4, skip 4 dc, 4 dc around ch loop, ch 4, 1 sc in the center of the 3 sc, ch 4*; rep from * to *across, ending with 4 dc around ch loop, ch 4, skip 4 dc, 1 sc around next ch loop, ch 4, skip 4 dc, 4 dc around ch loop, ch 2, 1 edc around same ch loop; turn.

Row 16: Ch 6, *4 dc around ch loop, ch 4, skip 4 dc, 1 sc around ch loop, 1 sc in sc, 1 sc around next ch loop, ch 4, skip 4 dc, 4 dc around next ch loop, ch 2*; rep from * to * across, ending with 1 edc on same ch loop; turn.

Row 17: Ch 6, 4 dc around ch loop, *ch 4, skip 4 dc, 1 sc around next ch loop, 1 sc in each of the 3 sc, 1 sc around next ch loop, ch 4, skip 4 dc, 4 dc around next ch loop*; rep from * to * across, ending with ch 2, 1 edc on same ch loop; turn.

Row 18: Ch 6, 4 dc around ch loop, *ch 2, skip 4 dc, 4 dc around ch loop, ch 4, 1 sc in each of the center 3 sc, ch 4, 4 dc around ch loop*; rep from * to * across, ending with ch 2, skip 4 dc, 4 dc around ch loop, ch 2, 1 edc into same ch loop; turn.

Row 19: Ch 6, *4 dc around ch loop, ch 2, skip 3 dc, 1 dc in dc, ch 2, skip 2 ch, 1 dc in dc, ch 2, skip 3 dc, 4 dc around ch loop, ch 4, 1 sc in the center of the 3 sc, ch 4*; rep from * to * across, ending with 4 dc around ch loop, ch 2, skip 3 dc, 1 dc in dc, ch 2, skip 2 ch, 1 dc in dc, skip 3 dc, 4 dc around ch loop, ch 2, 1 edc around same ch loop; turn.

Row 20: Ch 6, *4 dc around ch loop, ch 2, skip 3 dc, (1 dc in dc, ch 2, skip 2 ch) 3 times, 1 dc in dc, ch 2, skip 3 dc, 4 dc around ch loop, ch 2*; rep * to * across, ending with 1 edc around same ch loop; turn.

Row 21: Ch 6, *4 dc around ch loop, ch 2, skip 3 dc, (1 dc in dc, ch 2, skip 2 ch) 5 times, 1 dc in dc, ch 2, skip 3 dc*; rep from * to * across, ending with 4 dc around ch loop, ch 2, 1 edc around same ch loop; turn.

Row 22: Ch 6, 3 dc around ch loop, *1 dc each in next 3 dc, (1 dc in dc, ch 2, skip 2 ch) 7 times*; rep from * to * across, ending with 1 dc in each of next 3 dc, 3 dc around ch loop, ch 2, 1 edc around same ch loop; turn.

Row 23: Ch 6, 3 dc around ch loop, 1 dc in dc, ch 2, skip 2 dc, *1 dc each in next 3 dc, (1 dc in dc, ch 2, skip 2 ch) 7 times*; rep from * to * across, ending with 1 dc in each of next 4 dc, ch 2, skip 2 dc, 1 dc in dc, 3 dc around ch loop, ch 2, 1 edc around same ch loop; turn.

Row 24: Ch 6, 3 dc around ch loop, 1 dc in dc, ch 2, skip 2 dc, 1 dc in dc, ch 2, skip 2 ch, 1 dc in dc, *1 dc each in next 3 dc, (1 dc in dc, ch 2, skip 2 ch) 7 times*; rep from * to * across, ending with 1 dc in each of next 4 dc, ch 2, skip 2 ch, 1 dc in dc, ch 2, skip 2 dc, 1 dc in dc, 3 dc around ch loop, ch 2, 1 edc around same ch loop; turn.

Row 25: Ch 6, 3 dc around ch loop, 1 dc in dc, ch 2, skip 2 dc, 1 dc in dc, (ch 2, skip 2 ch, 1 dc in dc) 2 times, *1 dc each in next 3 dc, (1 dc in dc, ch 2, skip 2 ch) 7 times*; rep from * to * across, ending with 1 dc in each of next 4 dc, (ch 2, skip 2 ch, 1 dc in dc) 2 times, ch 2, skip 2 dc, 1 dc in dc, 3 dc around ch loop, ch 2, 1 edc around same ch loop; turn.

Row 26: Ch 6, 3 dc around ch loop, 1 dc in dc, ch 2, skip 2 dc, 1 dc in dc, (ch 2, skip 2 ch, 1 dc in dc) 3 times, *1 dc each in next 3 dc, (1 dc in dc, ch 2, skip 2 ch) 7 times*; rep from * to * across, ending with 1 dc in each of next 4 dc, (ch 2, skip 2 ch, 1 dc in dc) 3 times, ch 2, skip 2 dc, 1 dc in dc, 3 dc around ch loop, ch 2, 1 edc around same ch loop; turn.

Row 27: Ch 6, 3 dc around ch loop, 1 dc in dc, ch 2, skip 2 dc, 1 dc in dc, (ch 2, skip 2 ch, 1 dc in dc) 4 times, *1 dc each in next 3 dc, (1 dc in dc, ch 2, skip 2 ch) 7 times*; rep from * to * across, ending with 1 dc in each of next 4 dc, (ch 2, skip 2 ch, 1 dc in dc) 4 times, ch 2, skip 2 dc, 1 dc in dc, 3 dc around ch loop, ch 2, 1 edc around same ch loop; turn.

Row 28: Ch 6, 3 dc around ch loop, 1 dc in dc, ch 2, skip 2 dc, 1 dc in dc, (ch 2, skip 2 ch, 1 dc in dc) 5 times, *1 dc each in next 3 dc, (1 dc in dc, ch 2, skip 2 ch) 7 times*; rep from * to * across, ending with 1 dc in each of next 4 dc, (ch 2, skip 2 ch, 1 dc in dc) 5 times, ch 2, skip 2 dc, 1 dc in dc, 3 dc around ch loop, ch 2, 1 edc around same ch loop; turn.

Row 29: Ch 6, 3 dc around ch loop, 1 dc in dc, ch 2, skip 2 dc, 1 dc in dc, (ch 2, skip 2 ch, 1 dc in dc) 6 times, *1 dc each in next 3 dc, (1 dc in dc, ch 2, skip 2 ch) 7 times*; rep from * to * across, ending with 1 dc in each of next 4 dc, (ch 2, skip 2 ch, 1 dc in dc) 6 times, ch 2, skip 2 dc, 1 dc in dc, 3 dc around ch loop, ch 2, 1 edc around same ch loop; turn.

Row 30: Ch 6, 3 dc around ch loop, 1 dc in dc, *ch 4, skip 2 dc, 1 dc in dc, 2 dc around ch loop, 1 dc in dc, (ch 2, skip 2 ch, 1 dc in dc) 5 times, 2 dc around ch loop, 1 dc in dc*; rep from * to * across, ending with ch 4, skip 2 dc, 1 dc in dc, 3 dc around ch loop, ch 2, 1 edc around same ch loop; turn.

Row 31: Ch 6, 3 dc around ch loop, 1 dc in dc, *ch 4, skip 3 dc, 1 sc around ch loop, ch 4, skip 3 dc, 1 dc in dc, 2 dc around ch loop, 1 dc in dc, (ch 2, skip 2 ch, 1 dc in dc) 3 times, 2 dc around ch loop, 1 dc in dc*; rep from * to * across, ending with ch 4, skip 3 dc, 1 sc around ch loop, ch 4, skip 3 dc, 1 dc in dc, 3 dc around ch loop, ch 2, 1 edc around same ch loop; turn.

Row 32: Ch 6, 3 dc around ch loop, 1 dc in dc, *ch 4, skip 3 dc, 1 sc around ch loop, 1 sc in sc, 1 sc around ch loop, ch 4, skip 3 dc, 1 dc in dc, 2 dc around ch loop, 1 dc in dc, ch 2, skip 2 ch, 1 dc in dc, 2 dc around ch loop, 1 dc in dc*; rep from * to * across, ending with ch 4, skip 3 dc, 1 sc around ch loop, 1 sc in sc, 1 sc around ch loop, ch 4, skip 3 dc, 1 dc in dc, 3 dc around ch loop, ch 2, 1 edc around same ch loop; turn.

Row 33: Ch 6, 4 dc around ch loop, *ch 4, skip 4 dc, 1 sc around next ch loop, 1 sc in each of the 3 sc, 1 sc around next ch loop, ch 4, skip 4 dc, 4 dc around ch loop*; rep from * to * across, ending with ch 2, 1 edc around same ch loop; turn.

Row 34: Ch 6, 4 dc around next ch loop, *ch 4, skip 4 dc, 4 dc around ch loop, ch 4, 1 sc in each of the 3 center sc, ch 4, 4 dc around ch loop*; rep from * to * across, ending with ch 4, skip 4 dc, 4 dc around ch loop, ch 2, 1 edc around same ch loop; turn.

Row 35: Ch 6, 4 dc around ch loop, *ch 4, skip 4 dc, 1 sc around ch loop, ch 4, skip 4 dc, 4 dc around ch loop, ch 4, 1 sc in center of the 3 sc, ch 4, 4 dc around ch loop*; rep from * to * across, ending with ch 4, skip 4 dc, 1 sc around ch loop, ch 4, skip 4 dc, 4 dc around ch loop, ch 2, 1 edc around same ch loop; turn.

Row 36: Ch 6, *4 dc around ch loop, ch 4, skip 4 dc, 1 sc around ch loop, 1 sc in sc, 1 sc around ch loop, ch 4, skip 4 dc, 4 dc around ch loop, ch 2*; rep from * to * across, ending with 1 edc around same ch loop; turn.

Row 37: Ch 6, 4 dc around ch loop, *ch 4, skip 4 dc, 1 sc around next ch loop, 1 sc in each of the next 3 sc, 1 sc around ch loop, ch 4, skip 4 dc, 4 dc around ch loop; * rep from * to * across, ending with ch 2, 1 edc around same ch loop; turn.

Row 38: Ch 6, 4 dc around ch loop, *ch 4, skip 4 dc, 4 dc around ch loop, ch 4, 1 sc in each of the 3 center sc, 1 sc around next ch loop, ch 4, skip 4 dc, 4 dc around ch loop; * rep from * to * across, ending with ch 4, skip 4 dc, 4 dc around ch loop, ch 2, 1 edc around same ch loop; turn.

Row 39: Ch 6, *4 dc around ch loop, ch 4, skip 4 dc, 1 sc around ch loop, ch 4, skip 4 dc, 4 dc around ch loop, ch 4, 1 sc in center of the 3 sc, ch 4*; rep from * to * across, ending with 4 dc around ch loop, ch 4, skip 4 dc, 1 sc around ch loop, ch 4, skip 4 dc, 4 dc around ch loop ch 2, 1 edc around same ch loop; turn.

Row 40: Ch 6, *4 dc around ch loop, ch 4, skip 4 dc, 1 sc around ch loop, 1 sc in sc, 1 sc around next ch loop, ch 4, skip 4 dc, 4 dc around ch loop, ch 2*; rep from * to * across, ending with 1 edc around same ch loop; turn.

Row 41: Ch 6, 4 dc around ch loop, *ch 4, skip 4 dc, 1 sc around next ch loop, 1 sc in each of the 3 sc, 1 sc around next ch loop, ch 4, skip 4 dc, 4 dc around ch loop; * rep from * to * across, ending with ch 2, 1 edc around same ch loop; turn.

Repeat Rows 17-41 3 times.

Next, repeat Rows 17-30 once.

For the last row, work 1 hdc in each dc and 2 hdc around every ch loop. Continue directly along the side edge down to the tip with 4 sc on every ch loop, 3 sc in the tip st and then work 4 sc in every ch loop up the side.

FINISHING:

Pin out shawl to desired finished measurements. Dampen and let dry completely before removing pins.

Handbag

TUNISIAN
CROCHET

MEASUREMENTS:
Width and Length: approx. 12 x 12 in /
31 x 31 cm
Base: approx. 12 x 4 in / 31 x 10 cm
Sides: approx. 4 x 12 in / 10 x 31 cm

MATERIALS:
Yarn: CYCA #3, Marks & Kattens M&K Linen
(100% linen, 136 yd/124 m / 50 g)
Natural 952, 300 g

NOTIONS:
Leather handles
Thick posterboard and brown leather for base of
bag
Waxed linen thread

Tunisian Crochet Hook: U.S. size K-10½ /
6.5 mm
Crochet Hook: U.S. size H-8 / 5 mm for
foundation chain

GAUGE:
16 vertical sts with yarn held double and
Tunisian crochet hook = 4 in / 10 cm.
Adjust hook size to obtain correct gauge if
necessary.

1 pattern repeat (crossed stitches) = 2 sts

Crochet Stitches Used: Vertical sts and crossed
sts (see step-by-step guide for vertical sts on
page 122 and for crossed sts on page 124); chain
st (ch), slip st (sl st) (see pages 110-117).

INSTRUCTIONS:
FRONT AND BACK (make 2 pieces alike):
With smaller size crochet hook and yarn held
double, ch 53.
Row 1, forward: Change to larger size Tunisian
crochet hook. Beg in 2nd ch from hook, pick up
52 vertical sts in the top loop of each ch = 53 sts
on hook.
Row 1, return: Bind off all sts as follows: Yarn
around hook and through 1 loop, *yarn around
hook and though 2 loops*; rep from * to *
across.
Row 2, forward: 1 edge st, pick up 1 vertical st in
each vertical st across, ending with 1 edge st =
53 loops on hook.
Row 2, return: Bind off across as for Row 1,
return.
**Rows 3, forward and return, to 12, forward and
return:** Work as for Row 2, forward and return.
Row 13, forward: 1 edge st, *skip 1 vertical
st, pick up loop in next vertical st, go back to
skipped st and pick up loop in it—the stitches
will cross*; rep from * to * across, ending with 1
vertical st, 1 edge st = 53 loops on hook.
Row 13, return: Bind off all sts.
Row 14, forward: 1 edge st, 1 vertical st, *skip
1 vertical st, pick up loop in next vertical st, go
back to skipped st and pick up loop in it—the
stitches will cross*; rep from * to * across, ending with 1 edge st = 53 loops on hook.
Row 14, return: Bind off across.
Row 15, forward and return: Work as for Row 13,
forward and return.
Row 16, forward and return: Work as for Row 14,
forward and return.
Row 17, forward and return: Work as for Row 13,
forward and return.
Row 18, forward and return: Work as for Row 14,
forward and return.
Row 19, forward and return: Work as for Row 13,
forward and return.
Row 20, forward and return: Work as for Row 14,
forward and return.
**Rows 21, forward and return, to 50, forward and
return:** Work as for Row 2, forward and return.
With smaller size hook, bind off with sl st across
(see page 125).

BASE (make 1 piece):
With smaller hook and yarn held double, ch 53.
Row 1, forward: Change to larger size Tunisian
crochet hook. Beg in 2nd ch from hook, pick up
52 vertical sts in the top loop of each ch = 53
loops on hook.
Row 1, return: Bind off all sts as follows: Yarn

around hook and through 1 loop, *yarn around hook and though 2 loops*; rep from * to * across.

Row 2, forward: 1 edge st, pick up 1 vertical st in each vertical st across, ending with 1 edge st = 53 loops on hook.

Row 2, return: Bind off across as for Row 1, return.

Rows 3, forward and return, to 13, forward and return: Work as for Row 2, forward and return. With smaller size hook, bind off with sl st.

SIDES (make 2 pieces alike):
With smaller hook and yarn held double, ch 14.

Row 1, forward: Change to larger size Tunisian crochet hook. Beg in 2nd ch from hook, pick up 13 vertical sts in the top loop of each ch = 14 loops on hook.

Row 1, return: Bind off all sts as follows: Yarn around hook and through 1 loop, *yarn around hook and though 2 loops*; rep from * to * across.

Row 2, forward: 1 edge st, pick up 1 vertical st in each vertical st across, ending with 1 edge st = 14 loops on hook.

Row 2, return: Bind off across as for Row 1, return.

Rows 3, forward and return, to 50, forward and return: Work as for Row 2, forward and return. With smaller size hook, bind off with sl st.

FINISHING:
With RS facing out, crochet the bag together with yarn held double as follows: When all the pieces have been worked, seam the bag. Begin by joining the base and one side with WS facing WS and the side facing you. With smaller size hook, crochet the pieces together with 1 sl st in each edge st on the base and the bound off-edge of the side; cut yarn, leaving a somewhat long tail. Join the other side to the base the same way. Now crochet the front to the sides. Begin at the top of the bag with the front and side pieces, WS facing WS and the front facing you. Crochet the pieces together with 1 sl st in each edge st all the way down the side; cut yarn, leaving a somewhat long tail. With WS facing WS, join the base and front with the front facing you. Crochet together with 1 sl st in each bound-off/cast-on edge on the base and bound-off edge of the front; cut yarn, leaving a long tail. Now crochet the last side to the front with front facing you. Begin at the base and work up to the top edge, working 1 sl st in each edge st down the size; cut yarn, leaving a somewhat long tail.

Thread all the tails into the inside of the bag and tighten them. Knot them firmly together, thread onto tapestry needle, and weave them in securely on the WS of the bag.

TOP EDGE:
Hold the bag with the WS facing you and work 1 sl st in each st all the way around the edge (this round of sl sts reinforces the edging). Turn the bag right side out and work 1 sc in each st all the way around, ending with 1 sl st into the 1st sc. Cut yarn and weave in ends securely on WS.

SEWING ON HANDLES:
Measure to the center of the front and back and place a pin at each center point. Place the leather handles so they are centered on the bag front/back, with the top of each about   in / 1 cm down from the edging. Use the waxed linen thread to sew on the handles.

Cut the posterboard to match the shape and size of the base of the bag. Glue the dark brown leather onto both sides of the board. Place inside bag at base.

ALTERNATIVE TO LEATHER HANDLES:
With smaller hook and yarn held double, ch 90.

Row 1, forward: Change to larger Tunisian crochet hook. Beginning in 2nd ch from hook, pick up 1 vertical st in top loop of each ch across = 89 sc.

Row 1, return: Bind off all sts as follows: Yarn around hook and through 1 loop, *yarn around hook and though 2 loops*; rep from * to * across.

Row 2, forward: 1 edge st, pick up 1 vertical st in each vertical st across, ending with 1 edge st = 89 loops on hook.

Row 2, return: Bind off across as for Row 1, return.

Rows 3, forward and return, and 4, forward and return: Work as for Row 2, forward and return. With smaller size hook, bind off with sl st. Make another handle the same way.

Attach crocheted handles as for leather handles.

Pincushions

CROCHET

MEASUREMENTS:
Diameter: approx. 4 in / 10 cm

MATERIALS:
Pincushion with bobbles or stripes
Yarn: CYCA #1, Du Store Alpakka Dreamline Sky (70% baby alpaca, 30% silk, 128 yd/117 m / 25g)
Sky Blue DL303, 25 g
CYCA #0, Du Store Alpakka Dreamline Soul (68% baby alpaca, 32% nylon, 195 yd/178 m / 25g)
Heather Blue/Rose Tones DL212, 25 g

Striped pincushion
Yarn: CYCA #1, Sandnes Garn Mini Duett (55% cotton, 45% Merino wool, 191 yd/175 m / 50 g)
Blue-Gray 5962, 50 g
White 1002, 50 g
Beige 2441, 50 g

NOTIONS:
Pincushion with bobbles or stripes or striped pincushion:
2 buttons
fiber fill

Crochet Hook: U.S. size F-5 / 3.75 mm

GAUGE:
The gauge varies depending on the yarn used and the size of the crochet hook. Adjust hook size to obtain correct gauge if necessary.

Crochet Stitches Used: Chain st (ch), slip st (sl st), single crochet (sc), double crochet (dc), bobble (see pages 110-117).

( ) Repeat the sequence within parentheses the number of times specified after the end parenthesis.

NOTE: The pincushion with the bobbles is worked with one strand of each yarn held together.

These pincushions are made with yarn leftover from other projects in the book. You can mix all sorts of yarn. The size of the pincushion depends on the thickness of yarn you choose and the size crochet hook you use.

See pages 118-119 for step-by-step instructions for making the pincushions.

INSTRUCTIONS:
FRONT:
With one strand of each yarn held together, ch 7 and join into a ring with 1 sl st in the 1st ch.
Rnd 1: Ch 1, work 12 sc around ring, ending with 1 sl st to 1st ch.
Rnd 2: Ch 3 (= 1st dc), 1 dc in the same sc, *2 dc in next sc*; rep from * to * around, ending with 1 sl st to top of ch 3 = 24 dc.
Rnd 3: Ch 3 (= 1st dc), *2 dc in the same dc, 1 dc in dc*; rep from * to * around, ending with 2 dc in same st, 1 sl st in top of ch 3 = 36 sts.

Rnd 4: Ch 3 (= 1st dc), 1 dc in dc, *2 dc in the same dc, 1 dc in each of next 2 dc*; rep from * to * around, ending with 2 dc in same st, 1 sl st in top of ch 3 = 48 sts.

Rnd 5: Ch 1, 1 sc in each of next 3 dc, *1 bobble in dc (= 5 dc in same st and then decreased back to 1 st—see pages 116-117 for step-by-step instructions for bobbles), 1 sc in each of next 3 dc*; rep from * to * around, ending with 1 bobble, 1 sl st into 1st ch.

Rnd 6: Ch 3 (= 1st dc), 1 dc in each of next 2 dc, *2 dc in the same dc, 1 dc in each of next 3 dc*; rep from * to * around, ending with 2 dc in same st, 1 sl st in top of ch 3 = 60 sts; cut yarn.

BACK:

Work as for the front through Rnd 4.

Rnd 5: Ch 1, 1 sc in each dc around; end with 1 sl st to first ch.

Rnd 6: Work as for Rnd 6 of Front. Cut yarn.

(see pages 116-117 for step-by-step instructions for bobbles)

FINISHING:

Edging: Place front and back together with WS facing WS. With a doubled strand of Sky Blue, attach yarn with 1 sl st through both layers. With RS facing you, work 1 sc in each stitch, working through both pieces; leave an opening about 1¾-2 in / 4-5 cm wide. Stuff pincushion and finish crocheting to close opening.

With 4 strands of Sky Blue, partition the cushion. Thread tapestry needle with the 4 strands of yarn. Insert needle up through the center of the pincushion to the front, holding the yarn firmly, bring the yarn around the cushion and then insert needle once again from back to front in center of cushion; tighten yarn well. Make a total of 6 partitions the same way, spacing them evenly apart. Sew buttons to center front and back at the same time; tighten thread well and weave in ends to inside.

STRIPED PINCUSHION

Crochet with doubled yarn—2 strands of the same yarn with Sky or Soul, or use a single strand of Mini Duett.

FRONT:

With a doubled strand of Sky Blue or single strand of Blue-Gray, ch 7 and join into a ring with 1 sl st into 1st ch.

Rnd 1: Ch 1, work 12 sc around ring, and end with 1 sl st into 1st ch.

Rnd 2: Ch 3 (= 1st dc), 1 dc in the same sc, *2 dc in next sc*; rep from * to * around, ending with 1 sl st to top of ch 3 = 24 dc. Change to Heather Blue/Rose or White on the last step of the sl st.

Rnd 3: With Heather Blue/Rose or White, ch 3 (= 1st dc), *2 dc in the same dc, 1 dc in dc*; rep from * to * around, ending with 2 dc in same st, 1 sl st in top of ch 3 = 36 sts. Change to Sky Blue or Blue-Gray on the last step of the sl st.

Rnd 4: With Sky Blue or Blue-Gray, ch 3 (= 1st dc), 1 dc in dc, *2 dc in the same dc, 1 dc in each of next 2 dc*; rep from * to * around, ending with 2 dc in same st, 1 sl st in top of ch 3 = 48 sts. Change to Heather Blue/Rose or White on the last step of the sl st.

Rnd 5: With Heather Blue/Rose or White, ch 3 (= 1st dc), 1 dc in each of next 2 dc, *2 dc in the same dc, 1 dc in each of next 3 dc*; rep from * to * around, ending with 2 dc in same st, 1 sl st in top of ch 3 = 60 sts. Change to Sky Blue or Blue-Gray on the last step of the sl st.

Rnd 6: With Sky Blue or Blue-Gray, ch 3 (= 1st dc), 1 dc in each of next 3 dc, *2 dc in the same dc, 1 dc in each of next 4 dc*; rep from * to * around, ending with 2 dc in same st, 1 sl st in top of ch 3 = 72 sts.

BACK:

Work as for Front.

FINISHING:

Edging: Place front and back together with WS facing WS. With a doubled strand of Heather Blue/Rose or a single strand of Beige, attach yarn with 1 sl st through both layers. With RS facing you, work 1 sc in each stitch, working through both pieces; leave an opening about 1¾-2 in / 4-5 cm wide. Stuff pincushion and finish crocheting to close opening.

With 4 strands of Heather Blue/Rose or Beige, partition the cushion. Thread tapestry needle with the 4 strands of yarn. Insert needle up through the center of the pincushion to the front, hold the yarn firmly, bring the yarn around the cushion and then insert needle once again from back to front in center of cushion; tighten yarn well. Make a total of 6 partitions the same way, spacing them evenly apart. Sew buttons to center front and back at the same time; tighten thread well and weave in ends to inside.

Tip: Use a bit of rubber (from a rubber glove for example) and hold it around the needle when you bring the yarn thorough the pincushion. This makes it easier to pull the needle and yarn through.

Tunisian Crochet
Hook Case

MEASUREMENTS:

Approx. 7½ x 11½ in / 19 x 29 cm

MATERIALS:

Yarn: CYCA #3, Rowan Pima Cotton DK (100% cotton, 142 yd/130 m / 50 g)
Baltic Blue SH063, 50 g
Badger (gray) SH064, 50 g

Tunisian Crochet Hook: U.S. size I-9 / 5.5 mm
Crochet Hook: U.S. size 7 / 4.5 mm for foundation chain and for finishing

GAUGE:

22 vertical sts with Tunisian crochet hook = 4 in / 10 cm.
Adjust hook size to obtain correct gauge if necessary.

1 pattern repeat (vertical and twisted vertical stitches) = 2 sts

Crochet Stitches Used: Vertical sts, twisted vertical sts, eyelets (see step-by-step guide for vertical sts on page 122 and page 124 for twisted vertical sts and eyelets); chain st (ch) (see pages 110-117).

( ) Repeat the sequence within parentheses the number of times specified after the end parenthesis.

When changing colors, bring new color through on the last step of the last st of the previous row. This produces a "complete" color on the first st of the next row.

INSTRUCTIONS:

With regular crochet hook and Badger, ch 45 sts.
Row 1, forward: Change to Tunisian crochet hook. Beg in 2nd ch from hook, pick up 5 vertical loops in the top loop of foundation chain. Yarn around hook, skip 1 ch, (pick up 4 vertical loops, yarn around hook, skip 1 ch) 4 times, (pick up 5 vertical loops, yarn around hook, skip 1 ch) 2 times, pick up 5 vertical loops, 1 edge st.
Row 1, return: Bind off as follows: Yarn around hook and through the 1st st on the hook, *yarn around hook and through 2 sts*; rep from * to * across.
NOTE: The yarnovers are bound off as for a ch (see eyelet stitches, page 124).
Row 2, forward: 1 edge st, (pick up 4 vertical loops, yarn around hook, skip 1 ch) 5 times, (pick up 5 vertical loops, yarn around hook, skip 1 ch) 2 times, pick up 5 vertical loops, 1 edge st.
Row 2, return: Work as for Row 1, return.
Rows 3, forward and return, to 28, forward and return: Work as for Row 2, forward and return. Cut yarn and change to Baltic Blue on last step of last st on Row 28.
Rows 29, forward and return, to 57, forward and return: With Baltic Blue, work as for Row 2, forward and return.
Row 58, forward: 1 edge st, pick up *1 vertical st, 1 twisted vertical st*; rep * to * across, ending with 1 edge st.
Row 58, return: Bind off all sts across.
Rows 59, forward and return, to 80, forward and return: Work as for Row 58, forward and return. Cut yarn and change to Badger on the last step of last st on Row 80.
Row 81, forward: With Badger, work 1 edge st, pick up *1 vertical st*; rep * to * across, ending with 1 edge st.
Row 81, return: Bind off all sts across.
Rows 82, forward and return, to 88, forward and return: Work as for Row 81, forward and return. Finish with a row of slip sts across (see page 125), using crochet hook U.S. size 7 / 4.5 mm.

FINISHING:

Fold the gray section in over the blue section at Row 29. Make sure that the holes from the ch loops align on the gray and blue sections. With hook size 7 / 4.5 mm and Baltic Blue, beginning at the lower edge at the foldline, work 1 sl st through both chain st holes. Continue in sl st across to the pockets for the hooks. Securely fasten off the ends at the beginning and ending points.

Tip: If it is difficult to find the holes, insert a knitting needle through the holes and pull them open a bit so that the slip sts can be worked through them.

See step-by-step pictures on the next page.

JOINING AND EDGES:

With Baltic Blue and crochet hook U.S. size 7 / 4.5 mm, work a row of slip sts in the space between Rows 80 and 81. Cut yarn and weave in ends at each side. Work a row of slip sts in the vertical blocks of Row 88; cut yarn and weave in ends at each side.

Fold the edge up at Row 80 and then down on WS (= flap). Beginning at lower right side, crochet together with slip sts through both edge sts down the long side. Join the other long side the same way.

TIE CORDS:

Make 6 cords the same way.
With Badger and crochet hook U.S. size 7 / 4.5 mm, ch 20.

Row 1: Work 1 sl st in each ch across; cut yarn. Place 3 cords on each side of the hook case. Measure ¼ in / 0.5 cm down from the top edge and the same amount from the lower edge on right and left sides of case. Place a cord at each of these points. Place the last 2 cords at the top of the pockets. Sew on the cords securely and fasten off tightly.

Fill the case with Tunisian crochet hooks. Fold in and overlap the long edges and secure the case by tying the cords.

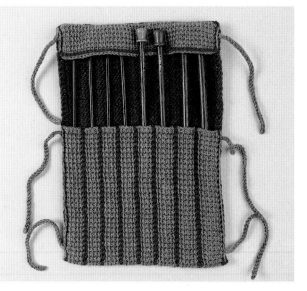

Crochet
Hook Case

CROCHET

MEASUREMENTS:
Approx. 10¾ x 7 in / 27 x 18 cm

MATERIALS:
Yarn: CYCA #3, Marks & Kattens M&K Linen
(100% linen, 136 yd/124 m / 50 g)
Blue 957, 50 g
Light Blue 964, 50 g

Crochet Hook: U.S. size D-3 / 3.25 mm;
U.S. size E-4 / 3.5 mm for foundation chain

GAUGE:
20 sc with smaller size hook = 4 in / 10 cm.
Adjust hook size to obtain correct gauge if
necessary.

1 pattern repeat (= 1 crochet hook pocket) =
5 sts

Crochet Stitches Used: Chain (ch) and slip
(sl) sts, single crochet (sc), half double crochet
(hdc), hdc worked through back loops, double
crochet (dc), crab st (see pages 110-117).

( ) Repeat the sequence within parentheses
the number of times specified after the end
parenthesis.

When changing colors, bring new color through
on the last step of the last st of the previous
row. This produces a "complete" color on the
first st of the next row.

The crochet hook case has pockets for 11
hooks. If you want storage for more hooks,
for each additional pocket, ch 5 extra sts. If
you want a smaller case, omit 5 ch for each
pocket less.

INSTRUCTIONS:
With Light Blue and larger hook, ch 59.
Row 1: Change to smaller size hook. Beginning
in 3rd ch from hook, work 1 hdc into each of the
next 5 ch, *ch 1, skip 1 ch, work 1 hdc in each of
next 4 ch*; rep * to * across, ending with 1 ch,
skip 1 ch, 1 hdc in each of next 6 ch; turn.
Row 2: Ch 2 (= 1 hdc), 1 hdc in each of next 5
hdc, *ch 1, skip 1 hdc, work 1 hdc in each of next
4 hdc*; rep * to * across, ending with ch 1, skip
1 hdc, 1 hdc each of next 6 hdc; turn.
Rows 3-19: Work as for Row 2. At the end of
Row 19, cut Light Blue and change to Blue on
the last st.
Row 20: With Blue, ch 2 (= 1 hdc), work 1 hdc
through back loop in each of next 5 hdc, *ch 1,
skip 1 hdc, work 1 hdc through back loop in each
of next 4 hdc*; rep * to * across, ending with ch
1, skip 1 hdc, work 1 hdc in back loop of each of
next 6 hdc; turn.
Rows 21-40: Work as for Row 20.
Row 41: Ch 3 (= 1 dc), 1 dc in each of next 5 hdc,
ch 1, skip 1 hdc, 1 dc in each of next 4 hdc;
rep * to * across, ending with ch 1, skip 1 hdc, 1
dc in each of next 6 hdc; turn.
Row 42: Ch 3 (= 1 dc), 1 dc in each of next 5 dc,
1 dc in ch loop, 1 dc in each of next 4 dc; rep
* to * across, ending with ch 1, skip 1 dc, 1 dc in
each of next 6 hdc; turn.
Row 43: Ch 1 (= 1 dc), 1 dc in each dc across; turn.
Rows 44-48: Work as for Row 43. At the end of
Row 48, cut Blue and change to Light Blue on
last st.
Row 49, Flap: With Light Blue, ch 1, 1 sc in back
loop of each dc across; turn.
Row 50: Ch 1, 1 sc through back loop in each sc
across; turn.
Rows 51-61: Work as for Row 50.
Row 62: 1 sl st in each sc across; cut yarn.

FINISHING:
Fold the Light Blue section over the Blue part at
Row 19. Make sure that the holes from the ch
loops align on the light blue and blue sections.
With Blue and smaller size hook, beginning at the
lower edge at the foldline, work 1 sl st through
both chain st holes. Continue in sl st across to
the pockets for the hooks. Securely fasten off
the ends at the beginning and ending points. See
step-by-step help on page 66.

Tip: If it is difficult to find the holes, insert a knitting needle through the holes and pull them open
a bit so that the slip sts can be worked through
them.

See step-by-step pictures on page 66.

JOINING AND EDGES:

Rnd 1: With Blue and smaller size hook, join the sides, beginning at lower edge of right side. Work sc across, with sts spaced as evenly as possible so that the edge doesn't pull in or ruffle. Continue in sc along the top edge to the beginning of th flap, work 3 sc in the corner st, work 1 sc in each dc of front section (the section that was not crocheted into at the color change to light blue), along the entire top edge, down left side as for right side, 3 sc at corner and then along lower edge to the fold, with 1 sc in each st, 3 sc in corner; end rnd with 1 sl st into 1st sc.

Rnd 2: Work 1 crab st in every sc around, changing to a smaller size hook if the edge is too loose. End rnd with 1 sl st into 1st crab st; cut yarn and fasten off securely.

TIE CORDS:

Make 4 cords the same way.
With Light Blue and smaller size hook, ch 30.
Row 1: Work 1 sl st in each ch across; cut yarn.

Place 2 cords on the left side of the hook case: measure 1½ in / 3.5 cm down from the top edge and the same amount from the lower edge. Place a cord at each of these points. Fold the case into thirds, folding in 3 pockets from the right side, and 4 pockets from the left side.
Place the other 2 cords at the fold on the right side, directly above the cords on the left side.
Sew on the cords securely and fasten off tightly.

Fill the case with crochet hooks. Fold the case into thirds and secure the case by tying the cords.

Afghan

CROCHET

MEASUREMENTS:
Approx. 44 x 63 in / 112 x 160 cm

MATERIALS:
Yarn: CYCA #4, Rowan Lima (84% baby alpaca, 8% Merino wool, 8% nylon, 120 yd/110 m / 50 g)
Cuzco (burgundy heather) 884, 250 g
Patagonia (dark blue) 878, 250 g
Amazon (blue) 879, 450 g
Andes (light gray-blue) 880, 250 g

Crochet Hook: U.S. size K-10½ / 6.5 mm

GAUGE:
1 pattern rep (12 sts) = 3¼ in / 8 cm.
Adjust hook size to obtain correct gauge if necessary.

1 pattern repeat = 12 sts

Crochet Stitches Used: Chain (ch), double crochet (dc), and double crochet decreases (dc dec) (see pages 110-117 and, for decreases, page 114).

( ) Repeat the sequence within parentheses the number of times specified after the end parenthesis.

When changing colors, bring new color through on the last step of the last st of the previous row. This produces a "complete" color on the first st of the next row.

INSTRUCTIONS:
With Amazon, ch 170.

Row 1: Work 1 dc in 4th ch from hook (the first 3 ch = 1 dc), 1 dc dec over next 2 ch, (2 dc in next ch) 4 times, *(1 dc dec over next 2 ch) 4 times, (2 dc in next ch) 4 times*; rep from * to * across, ending with (1 dc dec over next 2 ch) 2 times; turn.

Row 2: Ch 3, 1 dc in dc, 1 dc dec over next 2 dc, (2 dc in next dc) 4 times, *(1 dc dec over next 2 dc) 4 times, (2 dc in next dc) 4 times*; rep from * to * across, ending with 1 dc dec over next dc and top of ch 3; turn.

Row 3: Ch 3, 1 dc in dc, 1 dc dec over next 2 dc, (2 dc in next dc) 4 times, *(1 dc dec over next 2 dc) 4 times, (2 dc in next dc) 4 times*; rep from * to * across, ending with 1 dc dec over next 2 dc, 1 dc dec in next dc and top of ch 3; turn.

Rows 4-5: Work as for Row 2.

Row 6: Work as for Row 2, but change colors on last step of dc dec st at end of row: Cut Amazon and bring Andes through.

Row 7, with Andes: Work as for Row 2, but change colors on last step of dc dec at end of row: cut Andes and bring Patagonia through.

Row 8, with Patagonia: Work as for Row 2.

Row 9: Work as for Row 2, but change colors on last step of dc dec at end of row: Cut Patagonia and bring Andes through.

Row 10, with Andes: Work as for Row 2, but change colors on last step of dc dec at end of row: Cut Andes and bring Cuzco through.

Rows 11-13, with Cuzco: Work as for Row 2.

Row 14, with Cuzco: Work as for Row 2 but change colors on last step of dc dec at end of row: Cut Cuzco and bring Andes through.

Row 15 with Andes: Work as for Row 2, but change colors on last step of dc dec at end of row: Cut Andes and bring Patagonia through.

Row 16, with Patagonia: Work as for Row 2.

Row 17, with Patagonia: Work as for Row 2, but change colors on last step of dc dec at end of row: Cut Patagonia and bring Andes through.

Row 18, with Andes: Work as for Row 2, but change colors on last step of dc dec at end of row: Cut Andes and bring Amazon through.

Rows 19-23, with Amazon: Work as for Row 2.
Row 24, with Amazon: Work as for Row 2, but change colors on last step of dc dec st at end of row: Cut Amazon and bring Andes through.
Row 25, with Andes: Work as for Row 2.
Continue stitch pattern in the following color sequence:
6 rows Amazon
1 row Andes
2 rows Patagonia
1 row Andes

4 rows Cuzco
1 row Andes
2 rows Patagonia
1 row Andes
Repeat the stripe sequence 6 times and end the afghan with 6 rows Amazon (to match beginning of blanket).

FINISHING:
Weave in all ends neatly on WS. If necessary, lightly steam press on WS.

Romantic
Baby Blanket

MEASUREMENTS:
Approx. 39½ x 39½ in / 100 x 100 cm

MATERIALS:
Yarn: CYCA #1, Du Store Alpakka Dreamline Sky (70% baby alpaca, 30% silk, 128 yd/117 m / 25 g)
Natural White DL301, 75 g
Pink DL306, 100 g
Old Rose DL305, 150 g

Crochet Hook: U.S. size D-3 / 3.25 mm

GAUGE:
7 fans = 4 in / 10 cm.
Adjust hook size to obtain correct gauge if necessary.

1 pattern repeat = 5 sts

1 fan = (2 dc, ch 1, 2 dc) around the same ch loop of previous row

Crochet Stitches Used: Chain st (ch), slip st (sl st), double crochet (dc), treble crochet (tr) (see pages 110-113).

( ) Repeat the sequence within parentheses the number of times specified after the end parenthesis.

NOTE: Cut yarn and weave in end through back loops of sts on WS (see page 114).

INSTRUCTIONS:
With Natural White, ch 6 and join into a ring with sl st into 1st ch.

Rnd 1: Ch 3 (= 1st dc), 1 dc around ring, ch 1, 2 dc around ring, (ch 3, 2 dc around ring, ch 1, 2 dc around ring) 3 times. End rnd with ch 3, 1 sl st into 3rd ch at beg of rnd.

Rnd 2: 1 sl st into 1st dc, 1 sl st around ch, ch 3 (= 1st dc), 1 dc around ch, ch 1, 2 dc around same ch, *skip 2 dc, 2 dc around ch-3 loop, ch 2, 2 tr around same ch-3 loop, ch 2, 2 dc around same ch-3 loop (= corner), skip 2 dc, 2 dc around next ch, ch 1, 2 dc around same ch*; rep * to * 3 times. End with skip 2 dc, 2 dc around ch-3 loop, ch 2, 2 tr around same ch-3 loop, ch 2, 2 dc around same ch-3 loop (= corner), 1 sl st into top of ch 3. Cut yarn and weave in end along back loops of sts on WS.

Rnd 3: Change to Pink, attaching yarn with 1 sl st into ch of 1st fan of previous rnd. Ch 3 (= 1st dc), 1 dc around ch, ch 1, 2 dc around same ch, *skip 4 dc, 2 dc around ch-2 loop, ch 3, skip 2 tr (= corner), 2 dc around ch-2 loop, ch 1, 2 dc around same ch-2 loop, skip 4 dc, 2 dc around next ch, ch 1, 2 dc around same ch*; rep * to * 3 times. End with skip 4 dc, 2 dc around ch-2 loop, ch 1, 2 dc around same ch-2 loop, skip 2 tr, ch 3 (= corner), 2 dc around ch-2 loop, ch 1, 2 dc around same ch-2 loop, 1 sl st into top of ch 3 at beg of rnd.

Rnd 4: 1 sl st into 1st dc, 1 sl st around ch, ch 3 (= 1st dc), 1 dc around ch, ch 1, 2 dc around same ch, *skip 4 dc, 2 dc around ch, ch 1, 2 dc around same ch, skip 2 dc, 2 dc around ch-3 loop, ch 2, 2 tr around same ch-3 loop, ch 2, 2 dc around same ch-3 loop (= corner), skip 2 dc, 2 dc around ch, ch 1, 2 dc around same ch, skip 4 dc, 2 dc around same ch, ch 1, 2 dc around same ch*; rep * to * 3 times. End with skip 4 dc, 2 dc around ch, ch 1, 2 dc around same ch, skip 2 dc, 2 dc around ch-3 loop, ch 2, 2 tr around same ch-3 loop, ch 2, 2 dc around same ch-3 loop (= corner), skip 2 dc, 2 dc around ch, ch 1, 2 dc around same ch, 1 sl st into top of ch 3 at beg of rnd. Cut yarn and weave in end along back loops of sts on WS.

Rnd 5: Change to Old Rose, attaching yarn with 1 sl st into ch of 1st of previous rnd. Ch 3 (= 1st dc), 1 dc around ch, ch 1, 2 dc around same ch, *skip 4 dc, 2 dc around ch, ch 1, 2 dc around same ch, skip 4 dc, 2 dc around ch-2 loop, ch 1, 2 dc around same ch-2 loop, ch 3, skip 2 tr (= corner), 2 dc around ch-2 loop, ch 1, 2 dc around same ch-2 loop, (skip 4 dc, 2 dc around next ch, ch 1, 2 dc around same ch) 2 times*; rep * to * 3 times. End with skip 4 dc, 2 dc around ch, ch 1, 2 dc around same ch, skip 4 dc, 2 dc around ch-2 loop, ch 1, 2 dc around same ch-2 loop, ch 3, skip 2 tr (= corner), 2 dc around ch-2 loop, ch 1, 2 dc around same ch-2 loop, skip 4 dc, 2 dc around ch, ch 1, 2 dc around same ch, 1 st st into top of ch 3 at beg of rnd.

Rnd 6: 1 sl st into 1st dc, 1 sl st around ch, ch 3 (= 1st dc), 1 dc around ch, ch 1, 2 dc around same ch, *(skip 4 dc, 2 dc around ch, ch 1, 2 dc around same ch) 2 times, skip 2 dc, 2 dc around ch-3 loop, ch 2, 2 tr around same ch-3 loop, ch 2, 2 dc around same ch-3 loop (= corner), skip 2 dc, 2 dc around ch, ch 1, 2 dc around same ch, (skip 4 dc, 2 dc around ch, ch 1, 2 dc around same ch) 2 times*; rep * to * 3 times. End with (skip 4 dc, 2 dc around next ch, ch 1, 2 dc around same ch) 2 times, skip 2 dc, 2 dc around ch-3 ch loop, ch 2, 2 tr around same ch-3 loop, ch 2, 2 dc around same ch-3 loop (= corner), skip 2 dc, 2 dc around ch, ch 1, 2 dc around same ch, skip 4 dc, 2 dc around ch, ch 1, 2 dc around same ch, 1 sl st into top of ch 3 at beg of rnd. Cut yarn and weave in end along back loops of sts on WS.

Rnd 7: Change to Natural White, attaching yarn with sl st into ch on 1st fan of previous rnd. Ch 3 (= 1st dc), 1 dc around ch, ch 1, 2 dc around same ch, *(skip 4 dc, 2 dc around ch, ch 1, 2 dc around same ch) 2 times, skip 4 dc, 2 dc around ch-2 loop, ch 1, 2 dc around same ch-2 loop, skip 2 tr, ch 3 (= corner), 2 dc around ch-2 loop, ch 1, 2 dc around same ch-2 loop, (skip 4 dc, 2 dc around next ch, ch 1, 2 dc around same ch) 3 times*; rep * to * 3 times. End with (skip 4 dc, 2 dc around ch, ch 1, 2 dc around same ch) 2 times, skip 4 dc, 2 dc around ch-2 loop, ch 1, 2 dc around same ch-2 loop, skip 2 tr, ch 3 (= corner), 2 dc around ch-2 loop, ch 1, 2 dc around same ch-2 loop, (skip 4 dc, 2 dc around ch, ch 1, 2 dc around same ch) 2 times, 1 sl st into top of ch 3 at beg of rnd.

Rnd 8: 1 sl st into 1st dc, 1 sl st around ch 1, ch 3 (= 1st dc), 1 dc around ch, ch 1, 2 dc around same ch, *skip 4 dc, 2 dc around ch, ch 1, 2 dc around same ch) 3 times, skip 2 dc, 2 dc around ch-3 loop, ch 2, 2 tr around same ch-3 loop, ch 2, 2 dc around ch-3 loop (= corner), skip 2 dc, 2 dc around ch, ch 1, 2 dc around same ch, (skip 4 dc, 2 dc around next ch, ch 1, 2 dc around same ch) 3 times*; rep * to * 3 times. End with (skip 4 dc, 2 dc around ch, ch 1, 2 dc around same ch) 3 times, skip 2 dc, 2 dc around ch-3 loop, ch 2, 2 tr around same ch-3 loop, ch 2, 2 dc around same ch-3 loop (= corner), skip 2 dc, 2 dc around ch, ch 1, 2 dc around same ch, (skip 4 dc, 2 dc

around ch, ch 1, 2 dc around same ch) 2 times, 1 sl st into top of ch 3 at beg of rnd. Cut yarn and weave in end along back loops of sts on WS.

Rnd 9: Change to Pink, attaching yarn with sl st into ch on 1st fan of previous rnd. Ch 3 (= 1st dc), 1 dc around ch, ch 1, 2 dc around same ch, *(skip 4 dc, 2 dc around ch, ch 1, 2 dc around same ch) 3 times, skip 4 dc, 2 dc around ch-2 loop, ch 1, 2 dc around same ch-2 loop, skip 2 tr, ch 3 *(= corner), 2 dc around ch-2 loop, ch 1, 2 dc around same ch-2 loop, (skip 4 dc, 2 dc around next ch, ch 1, 2 dc around same ch) 4 times*; rep * to * 3 times. End with (skip 4 dc, 2 dc around ch, ch 1, 2 dc around same ch) 3 times, skip 4 dc, 2 dc around ch-2 loop, ch 1, 2 dc around same ch-2 loop, skip 2 tr, ch 3 (= corner), 2 dc around ch-2 loop, ch 1, 2 dc around same ch-2 loop, (skip 4 dc, 2 dc around next ch, ch 1, 2 dc around same ch) 3 times, 1 sl st into top of ch 3 at beg of rnd.

Rnd 10: 1 sl st into 1st dc, 1 sl st around ch 1, ch 3 (= 1st dc), 1 dc around ch, ch 1, 2 dc around same ch, *skip 4 dc, 2 dc around ch, ch 1, 2 dc around same ch) 4 times, skip 2 dc, 2 dc around ch-3 loop, ch 2, 2 tr around same ch-3 loop, ch 2, 2 dc around ch-3 loop (= corner), skip 2 dc, 2 dc around ch, ch 1, 2 dc around same ch, (skip 4 dc, 2 dc around next ch, ch 1, 2 dc around same ch) 4 times*; rep * to * 3 times. End with (skip 4 dc, 2 dc around ch, ch 1, 2 dc around same ch) 4 times, skip 2 dc, 2 dc around ch-3 loop, ch 2, 2 tr around same ch-3 loop, ch 2, 2 dc around same ch-3 loop (= corner), skip 2 dc, 2 dc around ch, ch 1, 2 dc around same ch, (skip 4 dc, 2 dc around ch, ch 1, 2 dc around same ch) 3 times, 1 sl st into top of ch 3 at beg of rnd. Cut yarn and weave in end along back loops of sts on WS.

Rnd 11: Change to Old Rose, attaching yarn with 1 sl st into ch on 1st fan of previous rnd. Ch 3 (= 1st dc), 1 dc around ch, ch 1, 2 dc around same ch, *(skip 4 dc, 2 dc around ch, ch 1, 2 dc around same ch) 4 times, skip 4 dc, 2 dc around ch-2 loop, ch 1, 2 dc around same ch-2 loop, skip 2 tr, ch 3 *(= corner), 2 dc around ch-2 loop, ch 1, 2 dc around same ch-2 loop, (skip 4 dc, 2 dc around next ch, ch 1, 2 dc around same ch) 5 times*; rep * to * 3 times. End with (skip 4 dc, 2 dc around ch, ch 1, 2 dc around same ch) 4 times, skip 4 dc, 2 dc around ch-2 loop, ch 1, 2 dc around same ch-2 loop, skip 2 tr, ch 3 *(= corner), 2 dc around ch-2 loop, ch 1, 2 dc around same ch-2 loop, skip 2 tr, ch 3 (= corner), 2 dc around ch-2 loop, ch 1, 2 dc around same ch-2 loop, (skip 4 dc, 2 dc around next ch, ch 1, 2 dc around same ch) 4 times, 1 sl st into top of ch 3 at beg of rnd.

Rnd 12: 1 sl st into 1st dc, 1 sl st around ch 1, ch 3 (= 1st dc), 1 dc around ch, ch 1, 2 dc around same ch, *(skip 4 dc, 2 dc around ch, ch 1, 2 dc around same ch) 5 times, skip 2 dc, 2 dc around ch-3 loop, ch 2, 2 tr around same ch-3 loop, ch 2, 2 dc around same ch-3 loop (= corner), skip 2 dc, 2 dc around ch, ch 1, 2 dc around same ch, (skip 4 dc, 2 dc around next ch, ch 1, 2 dc around same ch) 5 times*; rep * to * 3 times. End with (skip 4 dc, 2 dc around ch, ch 1, 2 dc around same ch) 5 times, skip 2 dc, 2 dc around ch-3 loop, ch 2, 2 tr around same ch-3 loop, ch 2, 2 dc around same ch-3 loop (= corner), skip 2 dc, 2 dc around ch, ch 1, 2 dc around same ch, (skip 4 dc, 2 dc around ch, ch 1, 2 dc around same ch) 4 times, 1 sl st into top of ch 3 at beg of rnd. Cut yarn and weave in end along back loops of sts on WS.

Rnd 13: Change to Natural White, attaching yarn with 1 sl st into ch on 1st fan of previous rnd. Ch 3 (= 1st dc), 1 dc around ch, ch 1, 2 dc around same ch, *(skip 4 dc, 2 dc around ch, ch 1, 2 dc around same ch) 5 times, skip 4 dc, 2 dc around ch-2 loop, ch 1, 2 dc around same ch-2 loop, skip 2 tr, ch 3 (= corner), 2 dc around ch-2 loop, ch 1, 2 dc around same ch-2 loop, (skip 4 dc, 2 dc around next ch, ch 1, 2 dc around same ch) 6 times*; rep * to * 3 times. End with (skip 4 dc, 2 dc around ch, ch 1, 2 dc around same ch) 5 times, skip 4 dc, 2 dc around ch-2 loop, ch 1, 2 dc around same ch-2 loop, skip 2 tr, ch 3 (= corner), 2 dc around ch-2 loop, ch 1, 2 dc around same ch-2 loop, (skip 4 dc, 2 dc around next ch, ch 1, 2 dc around same ch) 5 times, 1 sl st into top of ch 3 at beg of rnd.

Rnd 14: 1 sl st into 1st dc, 1 sl st around ch 1, ch 3 (= 1st dc), 1 dc around ch, ch 1, 2 dc around same ch, *(skip 4 dc, 2 dc around ch, ch 1, 2 dc around same ch) 6 times, skip 2 dc, 2 dc around ch-3 loop, ch 2, 2 tr around same ch-3 loop, ch 2, 2 dc around same ch-3 loop (= corner), skip 2 dc, 2 dc around ch, ch 1, 2 dc around same ch, (skip 4 dc, 2 dc around next ch, ch 1, 2 dc around same ch) 6 times*; rep * to * 3 times. End with (skip 4 dc, 2 dc around ch, ch 1, 2 dc around same ch) 6 times, skip 2 dc, 2 dc around ch-3 loop, ch 2, 2 tr around same ch-3 loop, ch 2, 2 dc around same ch-3 loop (= corner), skip 2 dc, 2 dc around ch, ch 1, 2 dc around same ch, (skip 4 dc, 2 dc around ch, ch 1, 2 dc around same ch) 5 times, 1 sl st into top of ch 3 at beg of rnd. Cut yarn and weave in end along back loops of sts on WS.

Row 15: Change to Pink, attaching yarn with 1 sl st into ch on 1st fan of previous rnd. Ch 3 (= 1st

dc), 1 dc around ch, ch 1, 2 dc around same ch, *(skip 4 dc, 2 dc around ch, ch 1, 2 dc around same ch) 6 times, skip 4 dc, 2 dc around ch-2 loop, ch 1, 2 dc around same ch-2 loop, skip 2 tr, ch 3 (= corner), 2 dc around ch-2 loop, ch 1, 2 dc around same ch-2 loop, (skip 4 dc, 2 dc around next ch, ch 1, 2 dc around same ch) 7 times*; rep * to * 3 times. End with (skip 4 dc, 2 dc around ch, ch 1, 2 dc around same ch) 6 times, skip 4 dc, 2 dc around ch-2 loop, ch 1, 2 dc around same ch-2 loop, skip 2 tr, ch 3 (= corner), 2 dc around ch-2 loop, ch 1, 2 dc around same ch-2 loop, (skip 4 dc, 2 dc around next ch, ch 1, 2 dc around same ch) 6 times, 1 sl st into top of ch 3 at beg of rnd.

Rnd 16: 1 sl st into 1st dc, 1 sl st around ch 1, ch 3 (= 1st dc), 1 dc around ch, ch 1, 2 dc around same ch, *(skip 4 dc, 2 dc around ch, ch 1, 2 dc around same ch) 7 times, skip 2 dc, 2 dc around ch-3 loop, ch 2, 2 tr around same ch-3 loop, ch 2, 2 dc around same ch-3 loop (= corner), skip 2 dc, 2 dc around ch, ch 1, 2 dc around same ch, (skip 4 dc, 2 dc around next ch, ch 1, 2 dc around same ch) 7 times*; rep * to * 3 times. End with (skip 4 dc, 2 dc around ch, ch 1, 2 dc around same ch) 7 times, skip 2 dc, 2 dc around ch-3 loop, ch 2, 2 tr around same ch-3 loop, ch 2, 2 dc around same ch-3 loop (= corner), skip 2 dc, 2 dc around ch, ch 1, 2 dc around same ch, (skip 4 dc, 2 dc around ch, ch 1, 2 dc around same ch) 6 times, 1 sl st into top of ch 3 at beg of rnd. Cut yarn and weave in end along back loops of sts on WS.

Rnd 17: Change to Old Rose, attaching yarn with 1 sl st into ch on 1st fan of previous rnd. Ch 3 (= 1st dc), 1 dc around ch, ch 1, 2 dc around same ch, *(skip 4 dc, 2 dc around ch, ch 1, 2 dc around same ch) 7 times, skip 4 dc, 2 dc around ch-2 loop, ch 1, 2 dc around same ch-2 loop, skip 2 tr, ch 3 (= corner), 2 dc around ch-2 loop, ch 1, 2 dc around same ch-2 loop, (skip 4 dc, 2 dc around next ch, ch 1, 2 dc around same ch) 8 times*; rep * to * 3 times. End with (skip 4 dc, 2 dc around ch, ch 1, 2 dc around same ch) 7 times, skip 4 dc, 2 dc around ch-2 loop, ch 1, 2 dc around same ch-2 loop, skip 2 tr, ch 3 (= corner), 2 dc around ch-2 loop, ch 1, 2 dc around same ch-2 loop, (skip 4 dc, 2 dc around next ch, ch 1, 2 dc around same ch) 7 times, 1 sl st into 3rd ch at beg of rnd.

Rnd 18: 1 sl st into 1st dc, 1 sl st around ch 1, ch 3 (= 1st dc), 1 dc around ch, ch 1, 2 dc around same ch, *(skip 4 dc, 2 dc around ch, ch 1, 2 dc around same ch) 8 times, skip 2 dc, 2 dc around ch-3 loop, ch 2, 2 tr around same ch-3 loop, ch

2, 2 dc around same ch-3 loop (= corner), skip 2 dc, 2 dc around ch, ch 1, 2 dc around same ch, (skip 4 dc, 2 dc around next ch, ch 1, 2 dc around same ch) 8 times*; rep * to * 3 times. End with (skip 4 dc, 2 dc around ch, ch 1, 2 dc around same ch) 8 times, skip 2 dc, 2 dc around ch-3 loop, ch 2, 2 tr around same ch-3 loop, ch 2, 2 dc around same ch-3 loop (= corner), skip 2 dc, 2 dc around ch, ch 1, 2 dc around same ch, (skip 4 dc, 2 dc around ch, ch 1, 2 dc around same ch) 7 times, 1 sl st into top of ch 3 at beg of rnd. Cut yarn and weave in end along back loops of sts on WS.

Rnds 19-48: Repeat Rnds 17-18. On each round, add one more repeat of each sequence within parentheses. *At the same time*, work in color sequence of: 2 rnds Natural White, 2 rnds Pink, and 2 rnds Old Rose.

Rnds 49-56: Continue with Old Rose, adding one more rep of the sequences within parentheses on each rnd as set. Cut yarn and weave in end along back loops of sts on WS.

Rnd 57: With Pink, work the final rnd as for Rnd 17 (with extra repeats as set).

FINISHING:
Pin out afghan to finished measurements. Dampen blanket and block; do not remove wires or pins until blanket is completely dry.

Doll Blanket and Hat

Doll Blanket

MEASUREMENTS:
Approx. 13 x 17 in / 33 x 43 cm

MATERIALS:
Yarn: CYCA #1, Du Store Alpakka Fin (50% baby alpaca, 50% silk, 180 yd/165 m / 50 g)
Pink 217, 100 g
Off-White 201, 50 g

Crochet Hook: U.S. size D-3 / 3.25 mm; U.S. size E-4 / 3.5 mm for foundation chain

GAUGE:
23 sts in pattern with D-3 / 3.25 mm hook = 4 in / 10 cm.
Adjust hook size to obtain correct gauge if necessary.

1 pattern repeat = 8 sts

Crochet Stitches Used: Chain st (ch), slip st (sl st), single crochet (sc), double crochet (dc), front post and back post treble crochet (FPtr, BPtr) (see pages 110-113).

FP treble: Insert hook from front to back around post of dc or tr of row below.
BP treble: Insert hook from back to front around post of dc or tr of row below.
(see page 116)

INSTRUCTIONS:
With Pink and larger size hook, ch 75.
Row 1: Change to smaller size hook. Work 1 dc into 4th ch from hook (the first 3 ch = 1st dc), 1 dc in ch, *skip 2 ch, work 5 dc in next ch, skip 2 ch, work 3 dc in next ch*; rep * to * across, ending with skip 2 ch, 5 dc in next ch, skip 2 ch, 1 dc in each of next 2 ch; turn.
Row 2: Ch 3 (=1st dc), 1 dc in dc, *skip 2 dc, 5 dc in next st, skip 2 dc, 1 dc in dc, 1 FPtr around dc of row below, 1 dc in dc*; rep * to * across, ending with skip 2 dc, 5 dc in next st, skip 2 dc, 1 dc in each of next 2 dc; turn.
Row 3: Ch 3 (=1st dc), 1 dc in dc, *skip 2 dc, 5 dc in next st, skip 2 dc, 1 dc in dc, 1 BPtr, 1 dc in dc*; rep * to * across, ending with skip 2 dc, 5 dc in next st, skip 2 dc, 1 dc in each of next 2 dc; turn.
Row 4: Ch 3 (=1st dc), 1 dc in dc, *skip 2 dc, 5 dc in next st, skip 2 dc, 1 dc in dc, 1 FPtr, 1 dc in dc*; rep * to * across, ending with skip 2 dc, 5 dc in next st, skip 2 dc, 1 dc in each of next 2 dc; turn.
Repeat Rows 3-4 until blanket is 16 in / 41 cm long.

Edging: With Off-White and smaller size hook, attach yarn to a corner with 1 sl st, ch 3 (= 1st dc), 6 dc in corner, *skip 2 sts or 2 rows, 1 sc in next st, skip 2 sts or 2 rows, 7 dc in same st*; rep * to * around. Join with 1 sl st into first st.

FINISHING:
Weave in all ends neatly on WS. Steam press gently or block to finished measurements.

Doll Hat

MEASUREMENTS:
Circumference: approx. 10¼ in / 26 cm

MATERIALS:
Yarn: CYCA #1, Du Store Alpakka Fin (50% baby alpaca, 50% silk, 180 yd/165 m / 50 g)
Pink 217, 50 g
Off-White 201, 50 g or leftover yarn from blanket

Crochet Hook: U.S. size D-3 / 3.25 mm

GAUGE:
23 sts in pattern with D-3 / 3.25 mm hook = 4 in / 10 cm.
Adjust hook size to obtain correct gauge if necessary.

1 pattern repeat = 8 sts

Crochet Stitches Used: Chain st (ch), slip st (sl st), single crochet (sc), half double crochet (hdc), double crochet (dc) (see pages 110-113).

INSTRUCTIONS:
With Pink, ch 4 and join into a ring with 1 sl st into 1st ch.
Rnd 1: Ch 2 (= 1st hdc), work 9 hdc around ring and join with 1 sl st into top of beg ch.
Rnd 2: Ch 2 (= 1st hdc), 1 hdc in same st as ch 2, 2 hdc in each hdc around; end rnd with 1 sl st into top of beg ch = 20 hdc.
Rnd 3: Ch 3, 1 dc in same st as ch 3, 1 dc in each hdc around; end with 1 sl st into top of beg ch.
Rnd 4: Ch 2 (= 1st hdc), 1 hdc in same st as ch 2, 2 hdc in each dc around; end with 1 sl st into top of beg ch = 40 hdc).
Rnd 5: Work as for Rnd 3.
Rnd 6: Ch 2 (= 1st hdc), 1 hdc in same in same st as ch 2, 1 hdc in each of next 2 dc, *2 hdc in next dc, 1 hdc in each of next 2 dc*; rep * to * around, ending with 1 sl st into top of beg ch = 60 hdc.
Rnd 7: Work as for Rnd 3.
Rnd 8: Work as for Rnd 3 but with hdc instead of dc (beg with ch 3).
Rnds 9-17: Repeat Rnds 7-8. Cut yarn.
Rnd 18: With Off-White, work as for Rnd 3.
Rnd 19: Ch 1, 1 sc in each dc around; end with 1 sl st into 1st ch.
Rnds 20-22: Ch 1, 1 sc in each sc around; end with 1 sl st into 1st ch.
Rnd 23: Ch 3 (= 1st dc), skip 2 sc, work 5 dc in next sc, skip 2 sc, 1 dc in next sc*; rep * to * around and end with 1 sl st in last sc. Cut yarn.

FINISHING:
Weave in all ends neatly on WS. Lightly steam press hat. Ties (optional): With Off-White, twist 2 cords about 8 in / 20 cm long. Securely sew cords inside turned-up edge, approx. 1¼ in / 3 cm to each side of center back.

Princess Blanket

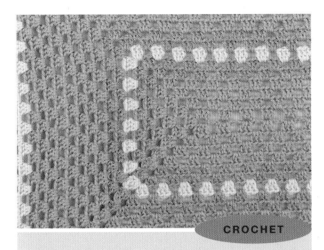

CROCHET

MEASUREMENTS:
Approx. 15¾ x 21 in / 40 x 53 cm

MATERIALS:
Yarn: CYCA #2, Du Store Alpakka BabySilk (80% baby alpaca, 20% silk, 145 yd/133 m / 50 g)
Pink 312, 100 g
Natural White 301, 50 g
Sand 324, 50 g

Crochet Hook: U.S. size E-4 / 3.5 mm;
U.S. size F-5 / 3.75 mm for foundation chain

GAUGE:
6 pattern repeats of 4 sts each (= 24 sts total) with hook E-4 / 3.5 mm = 4 in / 10 cm.
Adjust hook size to obtain correct gauge if necessary.

1 pattern repeat = 4 sts

Crochet Stitches Used: Chain st (ch), slip st (sl st), single crochet (sc), double crochet (dc), crab st (see pages 110-113).

( ) Repeat the sequence within parentheses the number of times specified after the end parenthesis.

When changing colors, begin on the last step of the last st of the previous row. This produces a "complete" color on the first st of the next row.

INSTRUCTIONS:
With Pink and larger size hook, ch 31 + ch 3 to begin 1st dc group = ch 34 total.

Rnd 1: Change to smaller size hook. Beginning in 4th ch from hook, work 2 dc, ch 3, 3 dc in same ch = first part of corner, ch 1, *skip 3 ch, 3 dc in next ch, ch 1*; rep * to * 6 times, skip 3 ch, (3 dc, ch 3, 3 dc, ch 3, 3 dc) in same ch = 2nd corner. Continue as set working along opposite side of foundation chain: ch 1, *skip 3 ch, 3 dc in same ch as dc group on opposite side, ch 1*; rep * to * 6 times, skip 3 ch, 3 dc in same ch as 1st part of first corner, ch 3; end rnd with 1 sl st into top of beg ch.

Rnd 2: (1 sl st in dc) 2 times, 1 sl st around ch loop, ch 3, (2 dc, ch 3, 3 dc) around ch loop, ch 1,*skip 3-dc group, 3 dc around ch loop, ch 1*; rep * to * 7 times, 3 dc, ch 3, 3 dc around next ch loop = corner, ch 1, 3 dc, ch 3, 3 dc around next ch loop = corner, ch 1, *skip 3-dc group, 3 dc around ch loop, ch 1*; rep * to * 7 times, 3 dc, ch 3, 3 dc around next ch loop = corner, ch 1; end rnd with 1 sl st into top of beg ch.

Rnd 3: (1 sl st in dc) 2 times, 1 sl st around ch loop, ch 3, (2 dc, ch 3, 3 dc) around ch loop, ch 1, *skip 3-dc group, 3 dc around ch loop, ch 1*; rep * to * 8 times, (3 dc, ch 3, 3 dc) around next ch loop = corner, ch 1, skip 3-dc group, 3 dc around ch loop, ch 1, (3 dc, ch 3, 3 dc) around next ch loop = corner, ch 1, *skip 3-dc group, 3 dc around ch loop, ch 1*; rep * to * 8 times, (3 dc, ch 3, 3 dc around next ch loop = corner, ch 1, skip 3-dc group, 3 dc around ch loop, ch 1; end rnd with 1 sl st into top of beg ch.

Rnd 4: (1 sl st in dc) 2 times, 1 sl st around ch loop, ch 3, (2 dc, ch 3, 3 dc) around ch loop, ch 1, *skip 3-dc group, 3 dc around ch loop, ch 1*; rep * to * 9 times, (3 dc, ch 3, 3 dc) around next ch loop = corner, ch 1, *skip 3-dc group, 3 dc around ch loop, ch 1)*; rep * to * 2 times, (3 dc, ch 3, 3 dc) around next ch loop = corner, ch 1, *skip 3-dc group, 3 dc around ch loop, ch 1*; rep * to * 9 times, (3 dc, ch 3, 3 dc around next ch loop = corner, ch 1, *skip 3-dc group, 3 dc around ch loop, ch 1*; rep * to * 2 times; end rnd with 1 sl st into top of beg ch. Cut yarn and weave in end in back loops of sts on WS (see page 114).

Rnd 5: Change to Sand, attaching yarn at a corner ch loop with 1 sc, ch 3, (2 dc, ch 3, 3 dc) around ch loop, ch 1, *skip 3-dc group, 3 dc around ch loop, ch 1*; rep * to * 10 times, (3 dc, ch 3, 3 dc) around next ch loop = corner, ch 1, *skip 3-dc group, 3 dc around ch loop, ch 1*; rep * to * 3 times, (3 dc, ch 3, 3 dc) around next ch loop = corner, ch 1, *skip 3-dc group, 3 dc around ch loop, ch 1*; rep * to * 10 times, (3 dc, ch 3, 3 dc) around next ch loop = corner, ch 1, *skip 3-dc group, 3 dc around ch loop, ch 1*; rep * to * 3 times. End with 1 sl st to top of beg ch.

Rnd 6: (1 sl st in dc) 2 times, 1 sl st around ch loop, ch 3, (2 dc, ch 3, 3 dc) around ch loop, ch 1, *skip 3-dc group, 3 dc around ch loop, ch 1*; rep * to * 11 times, (3 dc, ch 3, 3 dc) around next ch loop = corner, ch 1, *skip 3-dc group, 3 dc around ch loop, ch 1)*; rep * to * 4 times, (3 dc, ch 3, 3 dc) around next ch loop = corner, ch 1, *skip 3-dc group, 3 dc around ch loop, ch 1*; rep * to * 11 times, (3 dc, ch 3, 3 dc around next ch loop = corner, ch 1, *skip 3-dc group, 3 dc around ch loop, ch 1*; rep * to * 4 times; end rnd with 1 sl st into top of beg ch. Cut yarn and weave in end in back loops of sts on WS.

Rnd 7: Change to Natural White, attaching yarn at a corner ch loop with 1 sc, ch 3, (2 dc, ch 3, 3 dc) around ch loop, ch 1, *skip 3-dc group, 3 dc around ch loop, ch 1*; rep * to * 12 times, (3 dc, ch 3, 3 dc) around next ch loop = corner, ch 1, *skip 3-dc group, 3 dc around ch loop, ch 1*; rep * to * 5 times, (3 dc, ch 3, 3 dc) around next ch loop = corner, ch 1, *skip 3-dc group, 3 dc around ch loop, ch 1*; rep * to * 12 times, (3 dc, ch 3, 3 dc) around next ch loop = corner, ch 1, *skip 3-dc group, 3 dc around ch loop, ch 1*; rep * to * 5 times. End with 1 sl st to top of beg ch. Cut yarn and weave in end in back loops of sts on WS.

Rnd 8: Change to Sand, attaching yarn at a corner ch loop with 1 sc, ch 3, (2 dc, ch 3, 3 dc) around ch loop, ch 1, *skip 3-dc group, 3 dc around ch loop, ch 1*; rep * to * 13 times, (3 dc, ch 3, 3 dc) around next ch loop = corner, ch 1, *skip 3-dc group, 3 dc around ch loop, ch 1*; rep * to * 6 times, (3 dc, ch 3, 3 dc) around next ch loop = corner, ch 1, *skip 3-dc group, 3 dc around ch loop, ch 1*; rep * to * 13 times, (3 dc, ch 3, 3 dc) around next ch loop = corner, ch 1, *skip 3-dc group, 3 dc around ch loop, ch 1*; rep * to * 6 times. End with 1 sl st to top of beg ch.

Rnd 9: (1 sl st in dc) 2 times, 1 sl st around ch loop, ch 3, (2 dc, ch 3, 3 dc) around ch loop, ch 1, *skip 3-dc group, 3 dc around ch loop, ch 1*; rep * to * 14 times, (3 dc, ch 3, 3 dc) around next ch loop = corner, ch 1, *skip 3-dc group, 3 dc around ch loop, ch 1*; rep * to * 7 times, (3 dc, ch 3, 3 dc) around next ch loop = corner, ch 1, *skip 3-dc group, 3 dc around ch loop, ch 1*; rep * to * 14 times, (3 dc, ch 3, 3 dc) around next ch loop = corner, ch 1, *skip 3-dc group, 3 dc around ch loop, ch 1*; rep * to * 7 times; end rnd with 1 sl st into top of beg ch. Cut yarn and weave in end in back loops of sts on WS.

Rnd 10: Change to Pink, attaching yarn at a corner ch loop with 1 sc, ch 3, (2 dc, ch 3, 3 dc) around ch loop, ch 1, *skip 3-dc group, 3 dc around ch loop, ch 1*; rep * to * 15 times, (3 dc, ch 3, 3 dc) around next ch loop = corner, ch 1, *skip 3-dc group, 3 dc around ch loop, ch 1*; rep * to * 8 times, (3 dc, ch 3, 3 dc) around next ch loop = corner, ch 1, *skip 3-dc group, 3 dc around ch loop, ch 1*; rep * to * 15 times, (3 dc, ch 3, 3 dc) around next ch loop = corner, ch 1, *skip 3-dc group, 3 dc around ch loop, ch 1*; rep * to * 8 times. End with 1 sl st to top of beg ch.

Rnd 11: Continue as set, with 1 more dc-group on each of the 4 sides on every rnd.

Rnds 12-17: Work as for Rnd 11.

Rnds 18-19: Change to Natural White and work as for Rnd 11.

Rnds 20-22: Change to Sand and work as for Rnd 11.

Rnd 23: Change to Pink and work as for Rnd 11.

Rnd 24: (1 sl st in dc) 2 times, 4 sc around corner, *(1 sc in next dc) 3 times, 1 sc around ch *; rep * to * to next corner, (1 sc in next dc) 3 times, 4 sc around corner, rep * to * to next corner, (1 sc in next dc) 3 times, 4 sc around corner. Work last two sides as for first 2 sides and end with 1 sl st into 1st sc.

Rnd 25: Work 1 crab st into every sc around; end with 1 sl st into 1st crab st and cut yarn.

FINISHING:

Weave in remaining ends neatly on WS. Steam press or block blanket to finished measurements.

Doll Blanket

CROCHET

MEASUREMENTS:
Approx. 14¼ x 18¼ in / 36 x 46 cm

MATERIALS:
Yarn: CYCA #4, Rauma Chiri (55% baby alpaca, 22% superfine alpaca, 23% silk, 115 yd/105 m / 50 g)
Off-White 010, 100 g
Beige 071, 50 g

Crochet Hook: U.S. size G-6 / 4 mm;
U.S. size 7 / 4.5 mm for foundation chain

GAUGE:
17 hdc with hook G-6 / 4 mm = 4 in / 10 cm.
Adjust hook size to obtain correct gauge if necessary.

1 pattern repeat = 2 sts

Crochet Stitches Used: Chain st (ch), slip st (sl st), single crochet (sc), half double crochet (hdc), crab st (see pages 110-113)

The blanket is worked from one short side to the other.

INSTRUCTIONS:
With Off-White and larger size hook, ch 63.
Row 1: Change to smaller size hook. Beginning in 3rd ch from hook, work 1 hdc in each ch across; turn.
Row 2: Ch 2 (= 1st hdc), 1 hdc in each hdc across; turn.
Rows 3-9: Work as for Row 2.
Row 10: Ch 2 (= 1st hdc), *ch 1, skip 1 hdc, 1 hdc in hdc*; rep * to * across; turn.
Row 11: Ch 1, 1 sc in hdc, *1 sc around ch, 1 sc in hdc*; rep * to * across; turn.
Row 12: Ch 1 (= 1st sc), 1 sc in each sc across; turn.
Row 13: Work as for Row 12.
Now work in the following sequence:
Rep Rows 9-12.
Rep Rows 9-10.
Rep Row 2 9 times.
Rep Rows 9-12 5 times.
Rep Rows 9-10.
Rep Row 2 9 times.
Rep Rows 9-12 2 times.
Rep Rows 9-10.
Rep Row 2 9 times. Cut yarn.

Edging:
Rnd 1: With Beige and smaller size hook, work 1 sc in each st or row around, working 3 sc in each corner st; end with 1 sl st to 1st sc.
Rnd 2: Ch 1, work 1 crab st in each sc around; end with 1 sl st to 1st crab st. Cut yarn.

FINISHING:
Weave in all ends neatly on WS. Steam press or block blanket to finished measurements.

Blanket for a Prince

CROCHET

MEASUREMENTS:
Approx. 27½ x 31½ in / 70 x 80 cm

MATERIALS:
Yarn: CYCA #2, Du Store Alpakka BabySilk (80% baby alpaca, 20% silk, 145 yd/133 m / 50 g)
Natural White 301, 50 g
Light Blue 313, 100 g
Medium Blue 305, 100 g
Dark Blue 314, 150 g

Crochet Hook: U.S. size E-4 / 3.5 mm;
U.S. size F-5 / 3.75 mm for foundation chain

GAUGE:
7 pattern repeats of 4 sts each (= 28 sts total) with hook E-4 / 3.5 mm = 4 in / 10 cm.
Adjust hook size to obtain correct gauge if necessary.

1 pattern repeat = 4 sts

Crochet Stitches Used: Chain st (ch), slip st (sl st), single crochet (sc), double crochet (dc), crab st (see pages 110-113).

( ) Repeat the sequence within parentheses the number of times specified after the end parenthesis.

Tip: After cutting the yarn at the end of the round, hold the end on WS along the back loops of the sts and catch it as you work the new round (see step-by-step help on page 114).

INSTRUCTIONS:
With Natural White and larger size hook, ch 24; cut yarn.

Rnd 1: Change to smaller size hook and Light Blue. Ch 3 more in continuation of foundation chain. Beginning in 4th ch from hook (= 1st dc), work (2 dc, ch 1, 3 dc) in same ch = first part of corner, ch 1, *skip 3 ch, work 3 dc in same ch, ch 1*; rep * to * 5 times, skip 3 ch, work (3 dc, ch 1, 3 dc, ch 1, 3 dc) in same ch = corner. Continue on the opposite side of foundation chain: ch 1, *skip 3 ch, 3 dc in same st as dc-group on opposite side of foundation ch*; rep * to * 5 times, skip 3 ch, work 3 dc in same ch as first part of 1st corner, ch 1. End with 1 sl st into top of beg ch. Cut yarn.

Rnd 2: Attach Natural White with 1 sc around 1st ch 1 of corner, ch 3, skip 3 dc, 1 sc around next corner ch, ch 3, 1 sc around same corner ch, *ch 3, skip 3 dc, 1 sc around ch*; rep * to * 6 times, ch 3, skip 3 dc, 1 sc around corner ch, ch 3, 1 sc around same ch, ch 3, skip 3 dc, 1 sc around next corner ch, ch 3, 1 sc around same corner ch, *ch 3, skip 3 dc, 1 sc around ch*; rep to * 6 times, ch 3, skip 3 dc, 1 sc around corner ch, ch 3. End rnd with 1 st st into 1st sc. Cut yarn.

Rnd 3: Attach Medium Blue with 1 sl st to corner ch loop, ch 3, work (2 dc, ch 1, 3 dc) in same ch loop, ch 1, 3 dc around ch-3 loop, ch 1, skip 1 sc, 3 dc around next corner ch loop, ch 1, 3 dc around same corner ch loop, *ch 1, skip 1 sc, 3 dc around ch loop*; rep * to * 7 times, ch 1, **skip 1 sc, 3 dc around corner ch loop, ch 1, 3 dc around same corner ch loop**, ch 1, skip 1 sc, 3 dc around ch-3 loop, ch 1, skip 1 sc; rep ** to ** in next corner ch loop, *ch 1, skip 1 sc, 3 dc around ch-3 loop*; rep * to * 7 times, ch 1. End with 1 sl st into top of beg ch. Cut yarn.

Rnd 4: Attach Natural White with 1 sc around corner, ch 3, 1 sc around same ch loop, ch 3, **skip 3 dc, 1 sc around ch, ch 3**; rep ** to ** 2 times, skip 3 dc, 1 sc around next corner ch, ch 3, 1 sc around same corner ch, *ch 3, skip 3 dc, 1 sc around ch*; rep * to * 8 times, ch 3, skip 3 dc, 1 sc around corner ch, ch 3, 1 sc around same ch, ch 3, **skip 3 dc, 1 sc around ch, ch 3**; rep ** to ** 2 times, skip 3 dc, 1 sc around next corner ch, ch 3, 1 sc around same corner ch, *ch 3, skip 3 dc, 1 sc around ch*; rep to * 8 times. End with ch 3, skip 3 dc, 1 sc around corner ch, 1 st st into 1st sc. Cut yarn.

Rnd 5: Attach Dark Blue with 1 sl st to ch-3 loop at corner, ch 3, work (2 dc, ch 1, 3 dc) in same corner ch loop, *ch 1, skip 1 sc, 3 dc around ch-3 loop*; rep * to * 3 times, ch 1, skip 1 sc, 3 dc around next corner ch loop, ch 1, 3 dc around same corner ch loop, *ch 1, skip 1 sc, 3 dc around 3-ch loop*; rep * to * 9 times, ch 1, **skip 1 sc, 3 dc around corner ch loop, ch 1, 3 dc around same corner ch loop**, *ch 1, skip 1 sc, 3 dc around ch-3 loop*; rep * to * 3 times, ch 1, skip 1 sc; rep ** to ** in next corner, *ch 1, skip 1 sc, 3 dc around ch-3 loop*; rep * to * 9 times, ch 1. End with 1 sl st into top of beg ch. Cut yarn.

Rnd 6: Attach Natural White with 1 sc around corner ch, ch 3, 1 sc around same ch loop, **ch 3, skip 3 dc, 1 sc around ch**; rep ** to ** 4 times, ch 3, skip 3 dc, 1 sc around next corner ch, ch 3, 1 sc around same corner ch, *ch 3, skip 3 dc, 1 sc around ch*; rep * to * 10 times, ch 3, skip 3 dc, 1 sc around corner ch, ch 3, 1 sc around same ch, rep ** to ** 4 times, skip 3 dc, 1 sc around ch, ch 3, 1 sc around next corner ch, ch 3, 1 sc around same corner ch, *ch 3, skip 3 dc, 1 sc around ch*; rep * to * 10 times, ch 3, skip 3 dc. End rnd with 1 sl st into 1st sc. Cut yarn.

Rnd 7: Attach Light Blue with 1 sl st to ch-3 loop at corner, ch 3, work (2 dc, ch 1, 3 dc) in same corner ch loop, *ch 1, skip 1 sc, 3 dc around ch-3 loop*; rep * to * 5 times, ch 1, skip 1 sc, 3 dc around next corner ch loop, ch 1, 3 dc around same corner ch loop, *ch 1, skip 1 sc, 3 dc around 3-ch loop*; rep * to * 11 times, ch 1, **skip 1 sc, 3 dc around corner ch loop, ch 1, 3 dc around same corner ch loop**, *ch 1, skip 1 sc, 3 dc around ch-3 loop*; rep * to * 5 times, ch 1, skip 1 sc; rep ** to ** in next corner, *ch 1, skip 1 sc, 3 dc around ch-3 loop*; rep * to * 11 times, ch 1. End with 1 sl st into top of beg ch. Cut yarn.

Rnd 8: Attach Natural White with 1 sc around corner ch, ch 3, 1 sc around same ch loop, **ch 3, skip 3 dc, 1 sc around ch**; rep ** to ** 6 times, ch 3, skip 3 dc, 1 sc around next corner ch, ch 3, 1 sc around same corner ch, *ch 3, skip 3 dc, 1 sc around ch*; rep * to * 12 times, ch 3, skip 3 dc, 1 sc around corner ch, ch 3, 1 sc around same ch, rep ** to ** 6 times, skip 3 dc, 1 sc around ch, ch 3, 1 sc around next corner ch, ch 3, 1 sc around same corner ch, *ch 3, skip 3 dc, 1 sc around ch*; rep * to * 12 times, ch 3, skip 3 dc. End rnd with 1 sl st into 1st sc. Cut yarn.

Rnd 9: Attach Medium Blue with 1 sl st to ch-3 loop at corner, ch 3, work (2 dc, ch 1, 3 dc) in same corner ch loop, *ch 1, skip 1 sc, 3 dc around ch-3 loop*; rep * to * 7 times, ch 1, skip 1 sc, 3 dc around next corner ch loop, ch 1, 3 dc around same corner ch loop, *ch 1, skip 1 sc, 3 dc around 3-ch loop*; rep * to * 13 times, ch 1, **skip 1 sc, 3 dc around corner ch loop, ch 1, 3 dc around same corner ch loop**, *ch 1, skip 1 sc, 3 dc around ch-3 loop*; rep * to * 7 times, ch 1, skip 1 sc; rep ** to ** in next corner, *ch 1, skip 1 sc, 3 dc around ch-3 loop*; rep * to * 13 times, ch 1. End with 1 sl st into top of beg ch. Cut yarn.

Rnd 10: Attach Natural White with 1 sc around corner ch, ch 3, 1 sc around same ch loop, **ch 3, skip 3 dc, 1 sc around ch**; rep ** to ** 8 times, ch 3, skip 3 dc, 1 sc around next corner ch, ch 3, 1 sc around same corner ch, *ch 3, skip 3 dc, 1 sc around ch*; rep * to * 14 times, ch 3, skip 3 dc, 1 sc around corner ch, ch 3, 1 sc around same ch, rep ** to ** 8 times, skip 3 dc, 1 sc around ch, ch 3, 1 sc around next corner ch, ch 3, 1 sc around same corner ch, *ch 3, skip 3 dc, 1 sc around ch*; rep * to * 14 times, ch 3, skip 3 dc. End rnd with 1 sl st into 1st sc. Cut yarn.

Rnd 11: Attach Dark Blue with 1 sl st to ch-3 loop at corner, ch 3, work (2 dc, ch 1, 3 dc) in same corner ch loop, *ch 1, skip 1 sc, 3 dc around ch-3 loop*; rep * to * 9 times, ch 1, skip 1 sc, 3 dc around next corner ch loop, ch 1, 3 dc around same corner ch loop, *ch 1, skip 1 sc, 3 dc around 3-ch loop*; rep * to * 15 times, ch 1, **skip 1 sc, 3 dc around corner ch loop, ch 1, 3 dc around same corner ch loop**, *ch 1, skip 1 sc, 3 dc around ch-3 loop*; rep * to * 9 times, ch 1, skip 1 sc; rep ** to ** in next corner, *ch 1, skip 1 sc, 3 dc around ch-3 loop*; rep * to * 15 times, ch 1. End with 1 sl st into top of beg ch. Cut yarn.

Rnd 12: Attach Natural White with 1 sc around corner ch, ch 3, 1 sc around same ch loop, **ch 3, skip 3 dc, 1 sc around ch**; rep ** to ** 10 times, ch 3, skip 3 dc, 1 sc around next corner ch, ch 3, 1 sc around same corner ch, *ch 3, skip 3 dc, 1 sc around ch*; rep * to * 16 times, ch 3, skip 3 dc, 1 sc around corner ch, ch 3, 1 sc around same ch, rep ** to ** 10 times, skip 3 dc, 1 sc around ch, ch 3, 1 sc around next corner ch, ch 3, 1 sc around same corner ch, *ch 3, skip 3 dc, 1 sc around ch*; rep * to * 16 times, ch 3, skip 3 dc. End rnd with 1 sl st into 1st sc. Cut yarn.

Rnd 13: With Light Blue, work as for Rnd 11, working each repeat 2 more times.

Rnd 14: With Natural White, work as for Rnd 12, working each repeat 2 more times.
Rnd 15: With Medium Blue, work as for Rnd 13, working each repeat 2 more times.
Rnd 16: With Natural White, work as for Rnd 14, working each repeat 2 more times.
Rnd 17: With Dark Blue, work as for Rnd 15, working each repeat 2 more times.

Rep Rnds 12-17, each time working the repeats 2 more times. Continue until there are a total of 8 stripe sequence repeats or to desired size.

Edging:
Rnd 1: With Dark Blue and smaller size hook, begin with ch 3 and then work 1 dc in each dc around, skipping each ch st. At each corner, work 5 dc; end with 1 sl st in top of beg ch.
Rnd 2: Work 1 crab st in each dc around; end with 1 sl st into 1st crab st.

FINISHING:
Weave in all ends neatly on WS. Steam press or block blanket to finished measurements.

CROCHET

MEASUREMENTS:
Approx. 35½ x 39½ in / 90 x 100 cm

MATERIALS:
Yarn: CYCA #1, Du Store Alpakka
Dreamline Sky (70% baby alpaca, 30% silk,
128 yd/117 m / 25 g)
Sky Blue DL303, 275 g
Natural White DL301, 150 g

Crochet Hook: U.S. size D-3 / 3.25 mm; U.S.
size E-4 / 3.5 mm for foundation chain

GAUGE:
7 pattern repeats of 4 sts each (= 28 sts total),
on smaller size hook = 4 in / 10 cm.
Adjust hook size to obtain correct gauge if
necessary.

1 pattern repeat = 4 sts

Crochet Stitches Used: Chain st (ch), slip st
(sl st), single crochet (sc), double crochet (dc),
crab st (see pages 110-117).

( ) Repeat the sequence within parentheses
the number of times specified after the end
parenthesis.

NOTE: To fasten off yarn ends, weave in end
along back loops of sts on WS (see page 114).

Grandmother's Baby Blanket

INSTRUCTIONS:

With Blue and larger size hook, ch 24 + 3 for beg of 1st dc-group = 27 ch total.

Rnd 1: Change to smaller size hook. Beginning in 4th ch from hook, work (2 dc, ch 3, 3 dc) in same ch = 1st part of corner, ch 1, *skip 2 ch, 3 dc in same ch, ch 1*; rep * to * 5 times, skip 3 ch, (3 dc, ch 3, 3 dc, ch 3, 3 dc) in same ch = 2nd corner. Now continue along opposite side of foundation ch: ch 1, *skip 3 ch, 3 dc in same ch as dc-group on opposite side of foundation ch, ch 1*; rep * to * 5 times, skip 3 ch, 3 dc in same ch as first part of 1st corner, ch 3. End with 1 sl st into top of beg ch.

Rnd 2: (1 sl st in dc) 2 times, 1 sl st around ch loop, ch 3, (2 dc, ch 3, 3 dc) around ch loop, ch 1, *skip 3-dc group, 3 dc around ch loop, ch 1*; rep * to * 6 times, (3 dc, ch 3, 3 dc around next ch loop) = corner, ch 1, (3 dc, ch 3, 3 dc) around next ch loop = corner, ch 1, *skip 3-dc group, 3 dc around ch loop, ch 1*; rep * to * 6 times, (3 dc, ch 3, 3 dc) around next ch loop = corner, ch 1. End with 1 sl st into top of beg ch.

Rnd 3: (1 sl st in dc) 2 times, 1 sl st around ch loop, ch 3, (2 dc, ch 3, 3 dc) around ch loop, ch 1, *skip 3-dc group, 3 dc around ch loop, ch 1*; rep * to * 7 times, (3 dc, ch 3, 3 dc around next ch loop) = corner, ch 1, skip 3-dc group, 3 dc around ch loop, ch 1, (3 dc, ch 3, 3 dc) around next ch loop = corner, ch 1, *skip 3-dc group, 3 dc around ch loop, ch 1*; rep * to * 7 times, (3 dc, ch 3, 3 dc) around next ch loop = corner, ch 1, skip 3-dc group, 3 dc around ch loop, ch 1. End with 1 sl st into top of beg ch.

Rnd 4: (1 sl st in dc) 2 times, 1 sl st around ch loop, ch 3, (2 dc, ch 3, 3 dc) around ch loop, ch 1, *skip 3-dc group, 3 dc around ch loop, ch 1*; rep * to * 8 times, (3 dc, ch 3, 3 dc around next ch loop) = corner, ch 1, *skip 3-dc group, 3 dc around ch loop, ch 1*; rep * to * 2 times, (3 dc, ch 3, 3 dc) around next ch loop = corner, ch 1, *skip 3-dc group, 3 dc around ch loop, ch 1*; rep * to * 8 times, (3 dc, ch 3, 3 dc around next ch loop) = corner, ch 1, *skip 3-dc group, 3 dc around ch loop, ch 1*; rep * to * 2 times. End with 1 sl st into top of beg ch. Cut yarn and weave in end through back loops of sts on WS (see page 114).

Rnd 5: Attach Natural White with 1 sc around corner ch loop, ch 3, (2 dc, ch 3, 3 dc) around ch loop, ch 1, *skip 3-dc group, 3 dc around ch loop, ch 1*; rep * to * 9 times, (3 dc, ch 3, 3 dc around next ch loop) = corner, ch 1, *skip 3-dc group, 3 dc around ch loop, ch 1*; rep * to * 3 times, (3 dc, ch 3, 3 dc) around next ch loop = corner, ch 1, *skip 3-dc group, 3 dc around ch loop, ch 1*; rep * to * 9 times, (3 dc, ch 3, 3 dc around next ch loop) = corner, ch 1, *skip 3-dc group, 3 dc around ch loop, ch 1*; rep * to * 3 times. End with 1 sl st into top of beg ch.

Rnd 6: (1 sl st in dc) 2 times, 1 sl st around ch loop, ch 3, (2 dc, ch 3, 3 dc) around ch loop, ch 1, *skip 3-dc group, 3 dc around ch loop, ch 1*; rep * to * 10 times, (3 dc, ch 3, 3 dc around next ch loop) = corner, ch 1, *skip 3-dc group, 3 dc around ch loop, ch 1*; rep * to * 4 times, (3 dc, ch 3, 3 dc) around next ch loop = corner, ch 1, *skip 3-dc group, 3 dc around ch loop, ch 1*; rep * to * 10 times, (3 dc, ch 3, 3 dc around next ch loop) = corner, ch 1, *skip 3-dc group, 3 dc around ch loop, ch 1*; rep * to * 4 times. End with 1 sl st into top of beg ch.

Rnd 7: (1 sl st in dc) 2 times, 1 sl st around ch loop, ch 3, (2 dc, ch 3, 3 dc) around ch loop, ch 1, *skip 3-dc group, 3 dc around ch loop, ch 1*; rep * to * 11 times, (3 dc, ch 3, 3 dc around next ch loop) = corner, ch 1, *skip 3-dc group, 3 dc around ch loop, ch 1*; rep * to * 5 times, (3 dc, ch 3, 3 dc) around next ch loop = corner, ch 1, *skip 3-dc group, 3 dc around ch loop, ch 1*; rep * to * 11 times, (3 dc, ch 3, 3 dc around next ch loop) = corner, ch 1, *skip 3-dc group, 3 dc around ch loop, ch 1*; rep * to * 5 times. End with 1 sl st into top of beg ch. Cut yarn and fasten off (see page 114).

Rnd 8: Attach Blue with 1 sc around corner ch loop, ch 3, (2 dc, ch 3, 3 dc) around ch loop, ch 1, *skip 3-dc group, 3 dc around ch loop, ch 1*; rep * to * 12 times, (3 dc, ch 3, 3 dc around next ch loop) = corner, ch 1, *skip 3-dc group, 3 dc around ch loop, ch 1*; rep * to * 6 times, (3 dc, ch 3, 3 dc) around next ch loop = corner, ch 1, *skip 3-dc group, 3 dc around ch loop, ch 1*; rep * to * 12 times, (3 dc, ch 3, 3 dc around next ch loop) = corner, ch 1, *skip 3-dc group, 3 dc around ch loop, ch 1*; rep * to * 6 times. End with 1 sl st into top of beg ch.

Rnd 9: (1 sl st in dc) 2 times, 1 sl st around ch loop, ch 3, (2 dc, ch 3, 3 dc) around ch loop, ch 1, *skip 3-dc group, 3 dc around ch loop, ch 1*; rep * to * 13 times, (3 dc, ch 3, 3 dc around next ch loop) = corner, ch 1, *skip 3-dc group, 3 dc around ch loop, ch 1*; rep * to * 7 times, (3 dc, ch 3, 3 dc) around next ch loop = corner, ch 1, *skip 3-dc group, 3 dc around ch loop, ch 1*; rep * to * 13 times, (3 dc, ch 3, 3 dc around next ch loop) = corner, ch 1, *skip 3-dc group, 3 dc around ch loop, ch 1*; rep * to * 7 times. End with 1 sl st into top of beg ch.

Rnd 10: (1 sl st in dc) 2 times, 1 sl st around ch loop ch 3, (2 dc, ch 3, 3 dc) around ch loop, ch 1, *skip 3-dc group, 3 dc around ch loop, ch 1*; rep * to * 14 times, (3 dc, ch 3, 3 dc around next ch loop) = corner, ch 1, *skip 3-dc group, 3 dc around ch loop, ch 1*; rep * to * 8 times, (3 dc, ch 3, 3 dc) around next ch loop = corner, ch 1, *skip 3-dc group, 3 dc around ch loop, ch 1*; rep * to * 14 times, (3 dc, ch 3, 3 dc around next ch loop) = corner, ch 1, *skip 3-dc group, 3 dc around ch loop, ch 1*; rep * to * 8 times. End with 1 sl st into top of beg ch.

Rnd 11: (1 sl st in dc) 2 times, 1 sl st around ch loop, ch 3, (2 dc, ch 3, 3 dc) around ch loop, ch 1, *skip 3-dc group, 3 dc around ch loop, ch 1*; rep * to * 15 times, (3 dc, ch 3, 3 dc around next ch loop) = corner, ch 1, *skip 3-dc group, 3 dc around ch loop, ch 1*; rep * to * 9 times, (3 dc, ch 3, 3 dc) around next ch loop = corner, ch 1, *skip 3-dc group, 3 dc around ch loop, ch 1*; rep * to * 15 times, (3 dc, ch 3, 3 dc around next ch loop) = corner, ch 1, *skip 3-dc group, 3 dc around ch loop, ch 1*; rep * to * 9 times. End with 1 sl st into top of beg ch. Cut yarn and fasten off.

Rnd 12: Attach Natural White with 1 sc around corner ch loop, ch 3, (2 dc, ch 3, 3 dc) around ch loop, ch 1, *skip 3-dc group, 3 dc around ch loop, ch 1*; rep * to * 16 times, (3 dc, ch 3, 3 dc around next ch loop) = corner, ch 1, *skip 3-dc group, 3 dc around ch loop, ch 1*; rep * to * 10 times, (3 dc, ch 3, 3 dc) around next ch loop = corner, ch 1, *skip 3-dc group, 3 dc around ch loop, ch 1*; rep * to * 16 times, (3 dc, ch 3, 3 dc around next ch loop) = corner, ch 1, *skip 3-dc group, 3 dc around ch loop, ch 1*; rep * to * 10 times. End with 1 sl st into top of beg ch.

Rnd 13: (1 sl st in dc) 2 times, 1 sl st around ch loop, ch 3, (2 dc, ch 3, 3 dc) around ch loop, ch 1, *skip 3-dc group, 3 dc around ch loop, ch 1*; rep * to * 17 times, (3 dc, ch 3, 3 dc around next ch loop) = corner, ch 1, *skip 3-dc group, 3 dc around ch loop, ch 1*; rep * to * 11 times, (3 dc, ch 3, 3 dc) around next ch loop = corner, ch 1, *skip 3-dc group, 3 dc around ch loop, ch 1*; rep * to * 17 times, (3 dc, ch 3, 3 dc around next ch loop) = corner, ch 1, *skip 3-dc group, 3 dc around ch loop, ch 1*; rep * to * 11 times. End with 1 sl st into top of beg ch.

Rnd 14: (1 sl st in dc) 2 times, 1 sl st around ch loop, ch 3, (2 dc, ch 3, 3 dc) around ch loop, ch 1, *skip 3-dc group, 3 dc around ch loop, ch 1*; rep * to * 18 times, (3 dc, ch 3, 3 dc around next ch loop) = corner, ch 1, *skip 3-dc group, 3 dc around ch loop, ch 1*; rep * to * 12 times,

(3 dc, ch 3, 3 dc) around next ch loop = corner, ch 1, *skip 3-dc group, 3 dc around ch loop, ch 1*; rep * to * 18 times, (3 dc, ch 3, 3 dc around next ch loop) = corner, ch 1, *skip 3-dc group, 3 dc around ch loop, ch 1*; rep * to * 12 times. End with 1 sl st into top of beg ch. Cut yarn and fasten off.

Continue the same way, with 1 more 3-dc group on each side on every rnd. *At the same time*, continue the stripe sequence: 4 rnds Blue, 3 rnds Natural White. When 8 stripes total have been completed, cut Natural White and work edging.

Edging: Work 8 more rounds with Blue, increasing as set.

Next rnd: (1 sl st in dc) 2 times, 4 sc at corner, *(1 sc in dc) 3 times, 1 sc around ch*; rep * to * to next corner, ending with (1 sc in dc) 3 times, and then work 4 sc in corner ch; rep * to * to next corner, ending with (1 sc in dc) 3 times, 4 sc in corner ch. Work the other two sides the same way, ending with 1 sl st into 1st sc.

Last rnd: Work 1 crab st in each sc around; end with 1 sl st into 1st crab st. Cut yarn and fasten off.

FINISHING:

Weave in all ends neatly on WS. Steam press or block blanket to finished measurements.

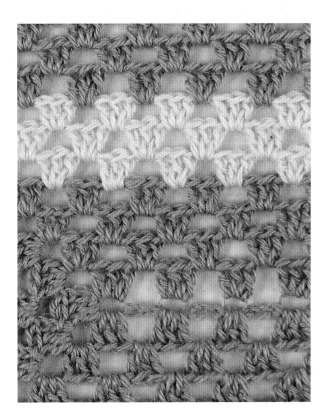

Striped Baby Blanket

CROCHET

MEASUREMENTS:
Approx. 17¾ x 24½ in / 45 x 62 cm

MATERIALS:
Yarn: CYCA #2, Du Store Alpakka BabySilk (80% baby alpaca, 20% silk, 145 yd/133 m / 50 g)
Light Blue 313, 200 g
Sand 324, 100 g

Crochet Hook: U.S. size E-4 / 3.5 mm;
U.S. size F-5 / 3.75 mm for foundation chain

GAUGE:
20 hdc with hook E-4 / 3.5 mm = 4 in / 10 cm.
Adjust hook size to obtain correct gauge if necessary.

1 pattern repeat = 2 sts

Crochet Stitches Used: Chain st (ch), slip st (sl st) single crochet (sc), half double crochet (hdc), crab st (see pages 110-113).

( ) Repeat the sequence within parentheses the number of times specified after the end parenthesis.

When changing colors, bring new color through on the last step of the last st of the previous row. This produces a "complete" color on the first st of the next row.

INSTRUCTIONS:
With Light Blue and larger size hook, ch 125.
Row 1: Change to smaller size hook. Beginning in 3rd ch from hook, work 1 hdc in each ch across; turn.
Row 2: Ch 2 (= 1st hdc), work 1 hdc in each hdc across; turn.
Rows 3-23: Work as for Row 2. Cut yarn and change to Sand on last st of Row 23; turn.
Row 24: Ch 2 (= 1st hdc), *ch 1, skip 1 hdc, 1 hdc in hdc*; rep * to * across; turn.
Row 25: Ch 1, 1 sc in hdc, *1 hdc around ch, 1 hdc in hdc*; rep * to * across; turn.
Row 26: Ch 2 (= 1st hdc), work 1 hdc in each hdc across; turn.
Row 27: Work as for Row 24. Cut yarn and change to Light Blue on last st of row; turn.
Row 28: Ch 1, 1 sc in hdc, *1 sc around ch, 1 sc in hdc*; rep * to * across; turn.
Row 29: Ch 2 (= 1st hdc), 1 hdc in each sc across. Cut yarn and change to Sand on last st of row; turn.
Rows 30-47: Work Rows 24-29 3 more times = 4 stripes each of Sand and Light Blue.
Rows 48-51: With Sand, work as for Rows 24-27. Change to Light Blue at end of Row 51.
Row 52: With Light Blue, work as for Row 28.
Row 53: Ch 2 (= 1st hdc), work 1 hdc in each sc across; turn.
Rows 54-76: Work as for Row 53 (working hdc into hdc). Cut yarn.

Edging:
Rnd 1: With Sand and smaller size hook, join yarn in a corner; ch 1 (= 1st sc), 2 sc, work 1 sc in each hdc along side and 3 sc in next corner, *as evenly as possible, work 3 sc for every 2 rows along short side*, 3 sc in corner, work 1 sc in each ch along foundation chain, 3 sc in corner, work * to * along other short side; end with 1 sl st into 1st sc.
Rnd 2: Beg at corner: Ch 3, 1 hdc in sc, ch 1, 1 hdc in next sc, ch 1, 1 sc in same sc, ch 1. Down long side: *skip 1 sc, 1 hdc in sc, ch 1*; rep * to * to corner. Skip 1 sc, [(1 hdc in sc, ch 1, 1 hdc) in same sc] 2 times; rep * to * to next corner. Skip 1 sc. [(1 hdc in sc, ch 1, 1 hdc) in same sc] 2 times; rep * to * to next corner. End with 1 sl st into 2nd ch.

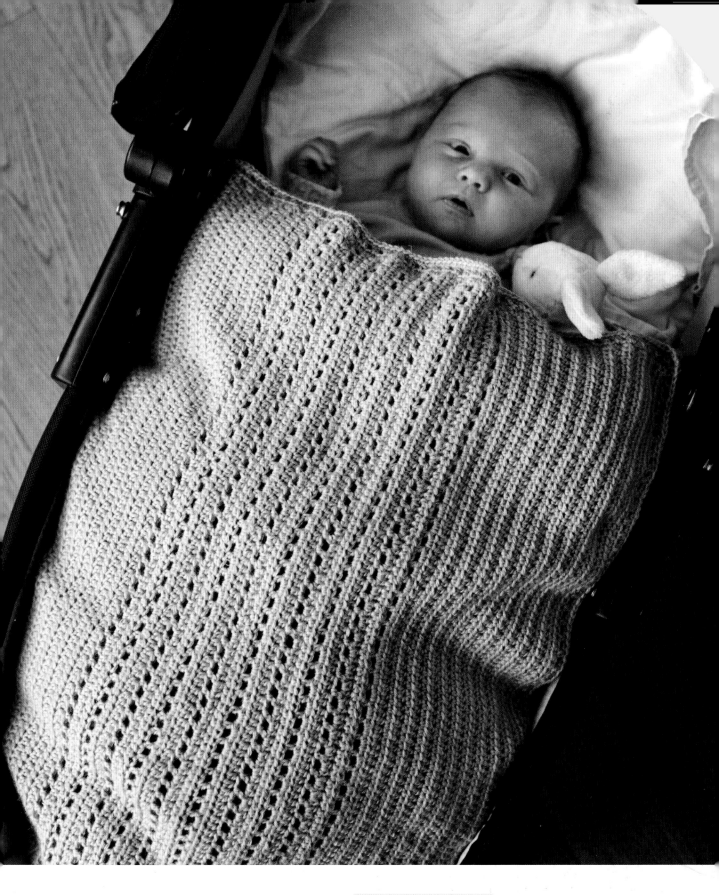

Rnd 3: Ch 1, *2 sc around ch, skip 1 hdc*; rep
* to * around and end with 1 sc into 1st ch. Cut
yarn and fasten off.

FINISHING:
Weave in all ends neatly on WS. Steam press or
block blanket to finished measurements.

Classic Shawl

CROCHET

MEASUREMENTS:
Approx. 35½ in / 90 cm as measured down center back to tip

MATERIALS:
Yarn: CYCA #1, SandnesGarn Mini Duett (55% cotton, 45% Merino wool, 191 yd/175 m / 50 g)
Blue-Gray 5962, 300 g
White 1002, 50 g
Beige 2441, 100 g

Crochet Hook: U.S. size F-5 / 3.75 mm

GAUGE:
20 sts in pattern = 4 in / 10 cm.
Adjust hook size to obtain correct gauge if necessary.

1 pattern repeat = 4 sts

Crochet Stitches Used: Chain st (ch), slip st (sl st), double crochet (dc), (see pages 110-113).

( ) Repeat the sequence within parentheses the number of times specified after the end parenthesis.

When changing colors, bring new color through on the last step of the last st of the previous row. This produces a "complete" color on the first st of the next row.

INSTRUCTIONS:
With Blue-Gray, ch 6 and join into a ring with 1 sl st into 1st ch.

Row 1: Ch 4, 2 dc around ring, ch 3, 3 dc around ring; turn.

Row 2: Ch 4, 2 dc in same st, skip 2 dc, ch 1, (3 dc, ch 3, 3 dc) around same ch-3 loop (= tip of shawl), ch 1, skip 2 dc, 3 dc in top of ch 4; turn.

Row 3: Ch 4, 2 dc in same dc, skip 2 dc, ch 1, 3 dc around ch, ch 1, skip 3 dc, (3 dc, ch 3, 3 dc) around same ch-3 ch loop (point of shawl), ch 1, skip 3 dc, 3 dc around ch, ch 1, skip 2 dc, work 3 dc in top of ch 4; turn.

Row 4: Ch 4, 2 dc in same dc, skip 2 dc, ch 1, (3 dc around ch, ch 1, skip 3 dc) 2 times, (3 dc, ch 3, 3 dc) around same ch-3 ch loop (point of shawl), (ch 1, skip 3 dc, 3 dc around ch) 2 times, ch 1, skip 2 dc, work 3 dc in top of ch 4; turn.

Row 5: Ch 4, 2 dc in same dc, skip 2 dc, ch 1, (3 dc around ch, ch 1, skip 3 dc) 3 times, (3 dc, ch 3, 3 dc) around same ch-3 ch loop (point of shawl), (ch 1, skip 3 dc, 3 dc around ch) 3 times, ch 1, skip 2 dc, work 3 dc in top of ch 4; turn.

Row 6: Ch 4, 2 dc in same dc, skip 2 dc, ch 1, (3 dc around ch, ch 1, skip 3 dc) 4 times, (3 dc, ch 3, 3 dc) around same ch-3 ch loop, (ch 1, skip 3 dc, 3 dc around ch) 4 times, ch 1, skip 2 dc, work 3 dc in top of ch 4, but, bring White through on last step of 3rd dc; cut Blue-Gray and turn.

Row 7, with White: Ch 4, 2 dc in same dc, skip 2 dc, ch 1, (3 dc around ch, ch 1, skip 3 dc) 5 times, (3 dc, ch 3, 3 dc) around same ch-3 ch loop, (ch 1, skip 3 dc, 3 dc around ch) 5 times, ch 1, skip 2 dc, work 3 dc in top of ch 4; turn.

Row 8: Ch 4, 2 dc in same dc, skip 2 dc, ch 1, (3 dc around ch, ch 1, skip 3 dc) 6 times, (3 dc, ch 3, 3 dc) around same ch-3 ch loop, (ch 1, skip 3 dc, 3 dc around ch) 6 times, ch 1, skip 2 dc, work 3 dc in top of ch 4, but, bring Beige through on last step of 3rd dc; cut White and turn.

Row 9, with Beige: Ch 4, 2 dc in same dc, skip 2 dc, ch 1, (3 dc around ch, ch 1, skip 3 dc) 7 times, (3 dc, ch 3, 3 dc) around same ch-3 ch loop, (ch 1, skip 3 dc, 3 dc around ch) 7 times, ch 1, skip 2 dc, work 3 dc in top of ch 4; turn.

Row 10: Ch 4, 2 dc in same dc, skip 2 dc, ch 1, (3 dc around ch, ch 1, skip 3 dc) 8 times, (3 dc, ch

3, 3 dc) around same ch-3 ch loop, (ch 1, skip 3 dc, 3 dc around ch) 8 times, ch 1, skip 2 dc, work 3 dc in top of ch 4; turn.

Row 11: Ch 4, 2 dc in same dc, skip 2 dc, ch 1, (3 dc around ch, ch 1, skip 3 dc) 9 times, (3 dc, ch 3, 3 dc) around same ch-3 ch loop, (ch 1, skip 3 dc, 3 dc around ch) 9 times, ch 1, skip 2 dc, work 3 dc in top of ch 4, but, bring Blue-gray through on last step of 3rd dc; cut Beige and turn.

Row 12, with Blue-Gray: Ch 4, 2 dc in same dc, skip 2 dc, ch 1, (3 dc around ch, ch 1, skip 3 dc) 10 times, (3 dc, ch 3, 3 dc) around same ch-3 ch loop, (ch 1, skip 3 dc, 3 dc around ch) 10 times, ch 1, skip 2 dc, work 3 dc in top of ch 4; turn.

Rows 13-19: Work as for Row 12, but, on every row, work 1 more repeat of each sequence with-in parentheses (not including tip which remains constant throughout). On Row 19, change to White on the last step of last st.

At the same time, work in the following color sequence:

2 rows White
3 rows Beige
8 rows Blue-Gray

Rep the stripe sequence 4 times, ending with 8 rows Blue-Gray (= a total of 16 rows of Blue-Gray at the outer edge of the shawl).

FINISHING:

Weave in ends neatly on WS. If necessary, lightly steam press to block.

Triangular Shawl

CROCHET

MEASUREMENTS:
Approx. 35½ in / 90 cm as measured down center back to tip

MATERIALS:
Yarn: CYCA #1, SandnesGarn Mini Duett (55% cotton, 45% Merino wool, 191 yd/175 m / 50 g) Khaki 3051, 350 g

Crochet Hook: U.S. size F-5 / 3.75 mm

GAUGE:
20 sts in pattern = 4 in / 10 cm.
Adjust hook size to obtain correct gauge if necessary.

1 pattern repeat = 4 sts

Crochet Stitches Used: Chain st (ch), slip st (sl st), single crochet (sc), half double crochet (hdc), double crochet (dc), treble crochet (tr) (see pages 110-113).

( ) Repeat the sequence within parentheses the number of times specified after the end parenthesis.

INSTRUCTIONS:
With Khaki, ch 6 and join into a ring with 1 sl st into 1st ch.

Row 1: Ch 4, 2 dc around ring, ch 3, 3 dc around ring; turn.

Row 2: Ch 4, 2 dc in same st, skip 2 dc, ch 1, (3 dc, ch 3, 3 dc) around same ch-3 loop (= tip of shawl), ch 1, skip 2 dc, 3 dc in top of ch 4; turn.

Row 3: Ch 4, 2 dc in same st, skip 2 dc, ch 1, 3 dc around ch, ch 1, skip 3 dc, (3 dc, ch 3, 3 dc) around same ch-3 loop (= tip of shawl), ch 1, skip 3 dc, 3 dc around ch, ch 1, skip 2 dc, 3 dc in top of ch 4; turn.

Row 4: Ch 4, 2 dc in same st, skip 2 dc, ch 1, (3 dc around ch, ch 1, skip 3 dc) 2 times, (3 dc, ch 3, 3 dc) around same ch-3 loop (= tip of shawl), (ch 1, skip 3 dc, 3 dc around ch) 2 times, ch 1, skip 2 dc, 3 dc in top of ch 4; turn.

Row 5: Ch 4, 2 dc in same dc, skip 2 dc, ch 1, (3 dc around ch, ch 1, skip 3 dc) 3 times, (3 dc, ch 3, 3 dc) around same ch-3 ch loop (point of shawl), (ch 1, skip 3 dc, 3 dc around ch) 3 times, ch 1, skip 2 dc, work 3 dc in top of ch 4; turn.

Row 6: Ch 4, 2 dc in same dc, skip 2 dc, ch 1, (3 dc around ch, ch 1, skip 3 dc) 4 times, (3 dc, ch 3, 3 dc) around same ch-3 ch loop, (ch 1, skip 3 dc, 3 dc around ch) 4 times, ch 1, skip 2 dc, work 3 dc in top of ch 4; turn.

Row 7: Ch 4, 2 dc in same dc, skip 2 dc, ch 1, (3 dc around ch, ch 1, skip 3 dc) 5 times, (3 dc, ch 3, 3 dc) around same ch-3 ch loop, (ch 1, skip 3 dc, 3 dc around ch) 5 times, ch 1, skip 2 dc, work 3 dc in top of ch 4; turn.

Row 8: Ch 4, 2 dc in same dc, skip 2 dc, ch 1, (3 dc around ch, ch 1, skip 3 dc) 6 times, (3 dc, ch 3, 3 dc) around same ch-3 ch loop, (ch 1, skip 3 dc, 3 dc around ch) 6 times, ch 1, skip 2 dc, work 3 dc in top of ch 4; turn.

Row 9: Ch 4, 2 dc in same dc, skip 2 dc, ch 1, (3 dc around ch, ch 1, skip 3 dc) 7 times, (3 dc, ch 3, 3 dc) around same ch-3 ch loop, (ch 1, skip 3 dc, 3 dc around ch) 7 times, ch 1, skip 2 dc, work 3 dc in top of ch 4; turn.

Row 10: Ch 4, 2 dc in same dc, skip 2 dc, ch 1, (3 dc around ch, ch 1, skip 3 dc) 8 times, (3 dc, ch 3, 3 dc) around same ch-3 ch loop, (ch 1, skip 3 dc, 3 dc around ch) 8 times, ch 1, skip 2 dc, work 3 dc in top of ch 4; turn.

Row 11: Ch 4, 2 dc in same dc, skip 2 dc, ch 1, (3 dc around ch, ch 1, skip 3 dc) 9 times, (3 dc, ch 3, 3 dc) around same ch-3 ch loop, (ch 1, skip 3 dc, 3 dc around ch) 9 times, ch 1, skip 2 dc, work 3 dc in top of ch 4; turn.

Row 12: Ch 4, 2 dc in same dc, skip 2 dc, ch 1, (3 dc around ch, ch 1, skip 3 dc) 10 times, (3 dc, ch 3, 3 dc) around same ch-3 ch loop, (ch 1, skip 3 dc, 3 dc around ch) 10 times, ch 1, skip 2 dc, work 3 dc in top of ch 4; turn.

Rows 13-62: Work as for Row 12, but, on every row, work 1 more repeat of each sequence within parentheses (not including tip, which remains constant throughout).

Row 63 (edging): *Ch 6, skip 3 dc, 1 sc around ch, skip 3 dc*; rep * to *across, ending with ch 6 in 3rd ch; turn.

NOTE: At the tip, work 1 sc around the ch-3 loop.

Row 64: Ch 8, *1 sc around ch loop, ch 6*; rep * to * across, ending with 1 sc around last ch loop, ch 4, 1 tr in same ch loop; turn.

Row 65: Ch 8, *1 sc around ch loop, ch 6*; rep * to * across, ending with 1 sc around last ch loop, ch 6, 1 sc around same ch loop; turn.

Row 66: *(2 sc, 1 hdc, 3 dc, 1 hdc, 2 sc) around same ch loop*; rep * to * across. Cut yarn.

FINISHING:

Weave in ends neatly on WS. If necessary, lightly steam press.

Cowl and Wrist Warmers

CROCHET

Cowl

MEASUREMENTS:
Length: approx. 9½ in / 24 cm
Circumference: approx. 23¾ in / 60 cm

MATERIALS:
Yarn: CYCA #3, Katia Basic Merino Flash (52% wool, 48% acrylic, 131 yd/120 m / 50 g) Blue-turquoise heather 806, 150 g

Crochet Hook: U.S. size 7 / 4.5 mm; U.S.size H-8 / 5 mm for foundation chain

GAUGE:
16 extended dc with smaller size hook = 4 in / 10 cm.
Adjust hook size to obtain correct gauge if necessary.

1 pattern repeat = 4 sts

Crochet Stitches Used: Chain st (ch), slip st (sl st), single crochet (sc), double crochet (dc), extended double crochet (edc), bobble (see pages 110-116).

( ) Repeat the sequence within parentheses the number of times specified after the end parenthesis.

Bobble: Work 5 dc into the same st but do not pull yarn through last step of each st = 6 loops on hook, yarn around hook and through all 6 loops (for step-by-step details, see page 116).

INSTRUCTIONS:
With larger size hook, ch 96 and join into a ring with 1 sl st into 1st ch.

Rnd 1: Change to smaller size hook. Ch 4 (= 1st edc), work 1 edc in each ch around = 96 edc; end with 1 sl st into top of beg ch.

Rnd 2: Ch 4 (= 1st edc), work 1 edc in each ch around = 96 edc; end with 1 sl st into top of beg ch.

Rnd 3: Ch 1, *(1 sc in edc) 3 times, 1 bobble in edc*; rep * to * around. End with 1 sl st into 1st sc.

Rnd 4: Ch 4 (= 1st edc), work 1 edc in each sc and bobble around; end with 1 sl st into top of beg ch.

Rnd 5: Ch 1, *1 sc in edc, 1 bobble in edc, (1 sc in edc) 2 times *; rep * to * around. End with 1 sl st into 1st sc.

Rnd 6: Ch 4 (= 1st edc), work 1 edc in each sc and bobble around; end with 1 sl st into top of beg ch.

Rnd 7: Ch 1, *(1 sc in edc) 3 times, 1 bobble in edc*; rep * to * around. End with 1 sl st into 1st sc.

Rnd 8: Ch 4 (= 1st edc), work 1 edc in each sc and bobble around; end with 1 sl st into top of beg ch.

Rnd 9: Ch 4 (= 1st edc), work 1 edc in each edc around; end with 1 sl st into top of beg ch.

Rnd 10: Work as for Rnd 9.
Rnd 11: Work as for Rnd 5.
Rnd 12: Work as for Rnd 6.
Rnd 13: Work as for Rnd 3.
Rnd 14: Work as for Rnd 6
Rnd 15: Work as for Rnd 5.
Rnd 16: Work as for Rnd 8.
Rnd 17: Work as for Rnd 9.
Rnd 18: Work as for Rnd 9.
Rnds 19-24: Work as for Rows 3-8.

Rnd 25 (eyelet rnd): Ch 4 (= 1 st edc), (1 edc in edc) 2 times, *ch 1, skip 1 edc, (1 edc in edc) 3 times; rep * to * around, ending with 1 sl st into top of ch 4.

Rnd 26: Ch 4 (= 1 st edc), (1 edc in edc) 2 times, *1 edc around ch, (1 edc in edc) 3 times*; rep * to * around, ending with 1 sl st into top of ch 4. Cut yarn.

CORD:
With larger size hook, ch 120. Change to smaller size hook and, beginning in 2nd ch from hook, work 1 sl st into each ch across.

FINISHING:
Weave in ends neatly on WS. Determine the center of the eyelet rnd and thread the cord through beginning at that point. Tie two knots at the end of the cord about ⅝ in / 1.5 cm from the end of the cord and the same spacing between the knots. Knot the opposite end of the cord the same way.

Wrist Warmers

MEASUREMENTS:
Length: approx. 6¼ in / 16 cm
Circumference: approx. 8 in / 20 cm

MATERIALS:
Yarn: CYCA #3, Katia Basic Merino Flash (52% wool, 48% acrylic, 131 yd/120 m / 50 g) Blue-turquoise heather 806, 50 g

Crochet Hook: U.S. size 7 / 4.5 mm

GAUGE:
16 extended dc = 4 in / 10 cm.
Adjust hook size to obtain correct gauge if necessary.

1 pattern repeat = 4 sts

Crochet Stitches Used: Chain st (ch), slip st (sl st), single crochet (sc), double crochet (dc), extended double crochet (edc), bobble (see pages 110-116).

( ) Repeat the sequence within parentheses the number of times specified after the end parenthesis.

Bobble: Work 5 dc into the same st but do put yarn through last step of each st = 6 loops on hook, yarn around hook and through all 6 loops (for more details, see page 116).

INSTRUCTIONS:
LEFT WRIST WARMER
Cuff: Ch 15.
Row 1: Beginning in 2nd ch from hook, work 1 sc in back loop of every ch = 14 sc; turn.
Rows 2-30: Ch 1, work 1 sc in back loop of every sc = 14 sc; turn.
Fold the cuff and crochet the last row to the first: *Insert hook through 1 sc and 1 ch of foundation ch and join with 1 sl st; rep from* across. Open cuff.
Now begin hand along the edge of the cuff.
Rnd 1: Ch 1, work 27 sc evenly spaced around edge of cuff; end with 1 sl st into 1st sc; turn.
Row 2: Thumbhole: Ch 4 (= 1 edc), (1 edc in sc) 26 times; turn.
Row 3: Ch 1, (1 sc in edc) 2 times, *1 bobble in edc, (1 sc in edc) 3 times*; rep * to * 3 times total, (1 sc in edc) 17 times, 1 sc in top of ch 4; turn.
Row 4: Ch 4 (= 1 edc), 1 edc in each sc and bobble across; turn.
Row 5: Ch 1, *1 bobble in edc, (1 sc in edc) 3 times*; rep * to * 4 times total, (1 sc in edc) 15 times, 1 sc in top of ch 4; turn.
Row 6: Work as for Row 4.
Row 7: Work as for Row 3 but end with 1 sl st into 1st sc.
Now work in the round:
Rnd 8: Ch 4 (= 1 edc), 1 edc in each sc and bobble across; end with 1 sl st into top of ch 4.
Rnd 9: Work as for Row 5 but do not turn. End 1 sl st into 1st bobble.
Rnd 10: Ch 4 (= 1 edc), 1 edc in each sc and bobble across; end with 1 sl st into top of ch 4.
Rnd 11: Ch 4 (= 1 edc), 1 edc in each edc across; end with 1 sl st into top of ch 4.
Rnd 12: Work 1 sc in each edc around; end with 1 sl st to 1st sc. Cut yarn.

RIGHT WRIST WARMER
Work cuff and Rnds 1-2 as for left wrist warmer.
Row 3: Ch 1: (1 sc in edc) 17 times, *1 bobble in edc, (1 sc in edc) 3 times *; rep * to * 3 times total, (1 sc in edc) 2 times, 1 sc in top of ch 4; turn.
Row 4: Ch 4 (= 1 edc), 1 edc in each sc and bobble across; turn.
Row 5: Ch 1, (1 sc in edc) 15 times, *(1 sc in edc) 3 times, 1 bobble in edc *; rep * to * 4 times total, 1 sc in top of ch 4; turn.
Row 6: Work as for Row 4.
Row 7: Work as for Row 3 but end with 1 sl st into 1st sc.
Now work around:

Rnd 8: Ch 4 (= 1 edc), 1 edc in each sc and bobble across; end with 1 sl st into top of ch 4.

Rnd 9: Work as for Row 5 but do not turn. End 1 sl st into 1st bobble.

Rnd 10: Ch 4 (= 1 edc), 1 edc in each sc and bobble across; end with 1 sl st into top of ch 4.

Rnd 11: Ch 4 (= 1 edc), 1 edc in each edc across; end with 1 sl st into top of ch 4.

Rnd 12: Work 1 sc in each edc around; end with 1 sl st to 1st sc. Cut yarn and weave in ends neatly on WS.

Large Cowl

CROCHET

MEASUREMENTS:
Length: approx. 9¾ in / 25 cm
Circumference: approx. 43¼ in / approx. 110 cm

MATERIALS:
Yarn: CYCA #3, Katia Basic Merino Flash (52% wool, 48% acrylic, 131 yd/120 m / 50 g) Rose/Purple heather 805, 150 g

Crochet Hook: U.S. size 7 / 4.5 mm; U.S. size H-8 / 5 mm for foundation chain

GAUGE:
16 extended dc with smaller size hook = 4 in / 10 cm.
Adjust hook size to obtain correct gauge if necessary.

1 pattern repeat = 3 sts

Crochet Stitches Used: Chain st (ch), slip st (sl st), extended double crochet (edc) (see pages 110–116).

( ) Repeat the sequence within parentheses the number of times specified after the end parenthesis.

INSTRUCTIONS:
With larger size hook, ch 228 and join into a ring with 1 sl st into 1st ch.

Rnd 1: Change to smaller size hook. (Ch 4 (= 1st edc), ch 1, 1 edc) in same ch, *skip 3 ch, (1 edc, ch 1, 1 edc) in same ch*; rep * to * around, ending with skip 3 ch, 1 sl st into top of ch 4.

Rnd 2: 1 sl st around ch, (ch 4 (= 1st edc), ch 1, 1 edc) in same ch, *skip 2 edc, (1 edc, ch 1, 1 edc) around same ch*; rep * to * around, ending with skip 2 edc, 1 sl st into top of ch 4.

Rnds 3-8: Work as for Rnd 2.

Rnd 9: 1 sl st around ch, (ch 4 (= 1st edc), 1 edc, ch 2, 2 edc) in same ch, *skip 2 edc, (2 edc, ch 2, 2 edc) around same ch*; rep * to * around, ending with skip 2 edc, 1 sl st into top of ch 4.

Rnd 10: Ch 1, skip 2 edc, 1 edc around ch loop, (ch 1, 1 edc around same ch loop) 3 times, ch 1, skip 2 edc, 1 sl st between 2nd and 3rd edc*; rep * to * around, ending with skip 2 edc, 1 sl st into 1st ch. Cut yarn.

Turn work so foundation chain faces you—the rest of the cowl is worked up from the foundation chain.

Rnd 11: Begin by attaching yarn with 1 sl st into a ch which has already been worked through; (ch 4 (= 1 edc), ch 1, 1 edc) in same ch, *skip 3 ch, (1 edc, ch 1, 1 edc) in same ch*; rep * to * around, ending with skip 3 ch, 1 sl st into top of ch 4.

Rnds 12-18: Work as for Rnd 2.

Rnd 19: Work as for Rnd 9.

Rnd 20: Work as for Rnd 10. Cut yarn.

FINISHING:
Weave in all ends neatly on WS.
You can wear the cowl very loosely around your neck or wrap it doubled around your neck for extra warmth.

Basic Instructions for Regular and Tunisian Crochet

Crochet

CROCHET TOOLS

To crochet, all you need is a hook the size appropriate for the yarn. Scissors and tapestry needles are also necessary for finishing and weaving in ends.

Crochet hooks are available in an assortment of materials: metal, plastic, bamboo, and wood. Wood hooks are my favorite because they fit well in my hand and are very comfortable to use. If you buy a crochet hook set with sizes U.S. D-3 to J-10 / 3 to 10 mm, you'll always have the right size on hand and you can easily find the one needed to suit your yarn and gauge.

BEGINNING OR ENDING A PIECE

Many patterns tell you to chain loosely. It's not always easy to do that and it's a good rule of thumb to use a larger size hook than that specified for the piece. For example, if the instructions say to use an H-8 / 5 mm hook, then working the foundation chain with a J-9 / 5.5 mm hook will produce an edge that doesn't pull in, an important factor for the look of the finished piece.

In the same vein, finish by working the final or last two rows or rounds with one U.S. size or one-half metric size smaller hook. Sometimes crochet work draws in a bit but you don't want that to happen on the last rows/rounds. If you worked the piece with an H-8 / 5 mm hook, then finishing with a US 7 / 4.5 mm will ensure that the edge will not be looser than the piece as a whole.

Tip: When you begin a piece with a lot of chain stitches, it's not always easy to keep count of the number of chains. To ensure that you have enough chains, make a few extra. You can undo any extra chains after you've worked the first row. Make sure that the knot at the beginning of the chain is not too tight. When there are extra chain sts, unpick the knot and then use a hook to undo the extra chain stitches. When you are even with the end of the first row, pull the yarn tail through firmly.

CROCHETING IN ROWS

When you get to the end of the first row across, turn the work. You can turn clockwise or counterclockwise. Decide how you want to turn and then work the same way throughout the piece. At the beginning of the next row, make the correct number of chain stitches (ch) to substitute for the first st (sc, dc, hdc, dc, tr, etc). Make 1 ch for a sc, 2 for a hdc, 3 for a dc, 4 for tr, and 5 for dbl tr.

CROCHETING IN THE ROUND

Instead of crocheting back and forth in rows, you can work in the round. Begin with the number of chain stitches specified in the instructions and then join into a ring with a slip stitch into the first chain loop. If you are going to make a flat disk, make sure that the increases are evenly spaced around throughout. If you are making a tube, crochet around and around without increasing. Each round begins with the same number of chain sts appropriate for the stitch (see Crocheting in Rows). End each round with a slip st into the first st of the round.

DIFFERENTIATING ROWS AND ROUNDS IN A PATTERN

When you crochet back and forth, you are working in rows.
When you crochet around, you are working in rounds.
Once you know if a piece is worked in rows or rounds, then you will understand how the piece is constructed. Sometimes both methods are used in one piece. For example, you might crochet the netting for a bag in the round but then work the handles back and forth.

JOINING YARN AND CHANGING COLORS

It is best to change or join yarn at the side of a piece or at the beginning of a round but sometimes that isn't possible. In that case, catch one yarn tail with the stitches as you crochet and catch the other yarn end on the next round or row. Tails can also be woven in during finishing by threading them into the backs of stitches with a tapestry needle.

Usually colors are changed at the beginning of a round or at the side. For a smooth transition between the colors, work as follows: before you begin the last stitch prior to the color change, make sure that the yarn to be dropped is on the wrong side of the piece. Crochet to the last yarnover on the stitch with the old color, yarn over hook with the new color and pull new color through on the last step of the stitch. Now continue with the new color. In this way, each of the stitches will be worked entirely in its own color.

CROCHET GAUGE

Each pattern specifies the gauge and you should make a swatch to test the gauge. Crochet a swatch about 6 x 6 in / 15 x 15 cm and take measurements within the center 4 x 4 in / 10 x 10 cm. Count the number of stitches and rows. It is important to make a gauge swatch bigger than 4 x 4 in / 10 x 10 cm because it will pull in a bit at the outer edges. If the stitch count doesn't match that in the pattern, change to a larger or smaller size hook. If there are too many stitches, change to a larger hook, and if there are too few stitches, use a smaller hook.

Tunisian Crochet

Tunisian crochet has several alternate names, such as Tunisian knitting or Afghan crochet. In this book, we'll use the term Tunisian crochet as it is the most common. The technique produces one of the sturdiest fabrics you can make so it is good for both placemats and potholders. The stitches won't unravel; each row consists of a forward and a return pass so each stitch is locked in. In order to work Tunisian crochet, you need a special Tunisian crochet hook. These hooks are long, straight, and even all down the shaft so you won't have any depression for holding onto the hook. The Tunisian crochet hook has to be long, with a stopper at one end so that there is enough room to hold all the stitches from a row without any falling off. Some Tunisian crochet hooks have a hook at each end so that you can work in the round. All of the Tunisian crochet projects in this book use a hook with a hook at only one end.

All Tunisian crochet projects begin with a chain stitch foundation that you can work with a regular crochet hook one size smaller than the Tunisian hook you'll use, to prevent the stitches from being too loose compared to the Tunisian crochet.

TUNISIAN CROCHET TOOLS

For Tunisian crochet, all you need is a Tunisian crochet hook the size appropriate for the yarn. Scissors and tapestry needles are also used for finishing and weaving in ends. Crochet hooks are available in an assortment of materials: metal, plastic, bamboo, and wood. Wood hooks are my favorite because they fit well in my hand and are very comfortable to use. As for regular crochet, you can buy a set of Tunisian crochet hooks in a range of sizes. It is also good to have a regular crochet hook for chaining the stitches at the beginning of a piece and for finishing.

Tip: When you begin a piece with a lot of chain stitches, it's not always easy to keep count of the number of chains. To ensure that you have enough chains, make a few extra. You can undo any extra chains after you've worked the first row. Make sure that the knot at the beginning of the chain is not too tight. When there are extra chain sts, unpick the knot and then use a hook to undo the extra chain stitches. When you are even with the end of the first row, pull the yarn tail through firmly.

TUNISIAN CROCHET ROWS

All of the completed rows in Tunisian crochet consist of two steps: a forward row and a return row.

TUNISIAN CROCHET GAUGE

Each pattern specifies the gauge and you should make a swatch to test the gauge. Crochet a swatch about 6 x 6 in / 15 x 15 cm and take measurements within the center 4 x 4 in / 10 x 10 cm. Count the number of stitches and rows. It is important to make a gauge swatch bigger than 4 x 4 in / 10 x 10 cm because it will pull in a bit at the outer edges. If the stitch count doesn't match that in the pattern, change to a larger or smaller size hook. If there are too many stitches, change to a larger hook and, if there are too few stitches, use a smaller hook.

BUY ENOUGH YARN

It is important to have enough yarn on hand before you start a piece. If you've already begun and have to buy more yarn, you may not be able to get the same dyelot and the colors won't match.

I also recommend that you always use good quality yarn to ensure the best results and the most enjoyable crocheting. The process is as important as the finished result!

ABBREVIATIONS AND GENERAL INFORMATION

Abbreviations

beg	begin, beginning
BP	back post—a stitch worked from the back around the post of another stitch
ch	chain
dc	double crochet (British: treble crochet)
dec	decrease
dtr	double treble crochet (British: triple treble crochet)
edc	extended double crochet
FP	front post—a stitch worked from the front around the post of another stitch
gr	group
hdc	half double crochet (British: half treble crochet)
rep	repeat
rnd	round
RS	right side
sc	single crochet (British: double crochet)
sl st	slip stitch
st(s)	stitch(es)
tc	turning chain
tog	together
tr	treble crochet (British: double treble crochet)
tr tr	triple treble crochet (British: quadruple treble crochet)
WS	wrong side
yo	yarnover/yarn around hook (British: yarn over hook/yoh)

Extended dc (edc): Yarn around hook, insert hook into st, yarn around hook, pull yarn through, yarn around hook, bring yarn through 1 loop on hook, *yarn around hook and bring through 2 loops on hook*; rep * to * 2 times (see pages 116-117).
NOTE: Substitute ch 3 for 1 edc at beginning of a row.

Dc group: Work the specified number of stitches (indicated before the words "dc-group") into the same stitch or around a chain loop; for example, a 3-dc group = 3 dc worked around the same stitch or chain loop.

Crab stitch = single crochet worked from left to right (see page 117).

Bobble = Work 1 dc up to the last time yarn is pulled through the stitch and leave the loop on the hook. Do the same with the next three stitches which are worked into the same stitch. Yarn around hook and through all the loops on the hook at the same time. Work 1 sc in the next st (the sc stabilizes the bobble) (see pages 116-117).

Front post dc (FPdc) = Yarn around hook and, beginning at front of work, insert hook behind the dc of previous row and out to front of work. Yarn around hook—there should now be 1 st, 1 yarnover, 1 dc and 1 yarnover on hook. Bring the last yarnover through, under the dc. Yarn around hook and complete the dc as usual. You can work either a front or a back post dc. When the dc is worked from the back, insert the hook around the dc of the previous round beginning from the back of the work. Other long stitches can also be worked through the front or back post, such as FPtr or BPtr tr.

Decreasing 1 dc (1 dc dec) = Work 1 dc but stop when there are 2 loops left on the hook. Work 1 dc into next st but stop when there are 3 loops left on the hook. Yarn around hook and bring through all 3 loops. Single crochet and half double crochet are decreased the same way (see page 114).

Increasing 1 dc = Work 2 dc into the same stitch. Single crochet and half double crochet are increased the same way (see page 115).

Check your gauge! If it is not correct, change hook size. If there are too many stitches in 4 in / 10 cm, use a larger hook; if there are too few stitches, use a smaller hook.

Chain Stitch (ch)

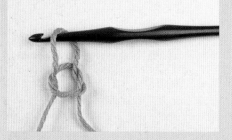  

STEP 1: Make a slip knot, insert hook into loop, and bring yarn from the ball through the loop with the hook; tighten yarn to firm up the loop around the hook.

STEP 2: Hold the hook in your right hand and the yarn over your left index finger. With yarn over the hook, bring hook through the loop already on hook and then you have a chain st (ch). Continue the same way until you have the desired number of stitches in the chain. Most crochet pieces begin with either a crochet foundation chain or ring.

STEP 3: If you are going to work with single crochet (sc), half double crochet (hdc), double crochet (dc), or treble crochet (tr), begin by inserting the hook into the chain st indicated in the pattern. First wrap the yarn the correct number of times around the hook for the stitch (the example here is once around the hook for a double crochet) and then insert the hook into the 4th chain from the hook and complete the stitch. The first 3 chain sts count as one dc.

Single Crochet (sc) through Both Loops

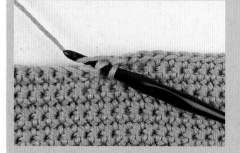  

STEP 1: Insert hook through both loops on top of stitch; yarn around hook.

STEP 2: Pull the yarn through both stitch loops.

STEP 3: Yarn around hook and through both loops on the hook.

NOTE: Slip stitches (sl st) are made as for single crochet but, in step 2, the yarn is pulled through the stitch and the loops on the hook at the same time. Slip stitches are used to join the end to the beginning of a round. You can also use slip stitches to taper the end so it isn't visible. Slip stitch all around the edge of a piece will make the edge firmer and stronger.

Single Crochet through Back Loops

STEP 1: Insert hook through the back loop of stitch, yarn around hook.

STEP 2: Pull the yarn through the back loop of the stitch.

STEP 3: Yarn around hook and through both loops on the hook.

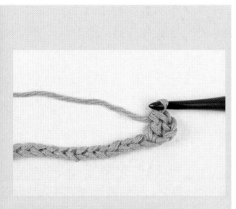

STEP 4: With yarn around hook, pull through the loops until the stitch is completed and then work across the foundation chain in pattern (the photos shows how a row of dc begins).

STEP 4: When only one loop remains on the hook, you've completed 1 sc; repeat Steps 1-3 for each single crochet.

STEP 4: When only one loop remains on the hook, you've completed 1 sc; repeat Steps 1-3 for each single crochet. Working single crochet into the back loops only produces a ribbed effect and a very elastic fabric. This stitch is a good substitute for ribbed edges.

Half Double Crochet (hdc) through Both Loops

STEP 1: Yarn around hook and insert hook through both loops on top of stitch; yarn around hook.

STEP 2: Pull the yarn through both stitch loops.

STEP 3: Yarn around hook and through all 3 loops on the hook.

Half Double Crochet through Back Loops

STEP 1: Yarn around hook, insert hook through the back loop of stitch, yarn around hook.

STEP 2: Pull the yarn through the back loop of the stitch.

STEP 3: Yarn around hook and through all 3 loops on the hook.

Double Crochet (dc)

STEP 1: Yarn around hook and insert hook through both loops at top of stitch, yarn around hook.

STEP 2: Pull the yarn through both stitch loops.

STEP 3: Yarn around hook (there are now 3 loops on hook), pull yarn through the first 2 loops on hook (2 loops now remain on hook). Yarn around hook and through both loops on hook.

NOTE: A double treble crochet (dbl tr) is worked the same way but begun with yarn around the hook 3 times; a triple treble crochet begins with yarn around the hook 4 times.

Treble Crochet (tr)

STEP 4: When only one loop remains on the hook, you've completed 1 hdc; repeat Steps 1-3 for each half double crochet.

STEP 1: Yarn around hook twice and insert hook through both loops at top of stitch; yarn around hook. Pull the yarn through both stitch loops.

STEP 2: Yarn around hook (there are now 4 loops on the hook) and pull yarn through the first 2 loops on hook (3 loops now remain on hook).

STEP 4: When only one loop remains on the hook, you've completed 1 hdc; repeat Steps 1-3 for each half double crochet. Working half double crochet through the back loops only produces a very elastic ribbed fabric, although single crochet through back loops makes a more elastic fabric and, thus, is better as a substitute for ribbing.

STEP 3: Yarn around hook and through two loops on hook (2 loops remain on hook). Yarn around hook; pull yarn through rem 2 loops on hook.

STEP 4: When only one loop remains on the hook, you've completed 1 tr; repeat steps 1-3 for each treble crochet.

STEP 4: When only one loop remains on the hook, you've completed 1 dc; repeat Steps 1-3 for each double crochet.

Changing Colors

STEP 1: On the last step of a stitch at the end of a row or round to be worked with a new color, do not bring the old color through remaining loops.

STEP 2: Wrap new color around the hook.

STEP 3: Bring the new color through the last 2 loops on the row or round.

Decreasing Stitches (photos show decreasing double crochet sts)

STEP 1: Work the given stitch up to the final step.

STEP 2: Work the next stitch on the row or round as given, up to the final step. You now have two half-finished stitches on the hook.

STEP 3: Yarn around hook and through remaining 3 loops = 1 st decreased.

Securing Yarn Ends through Back Loops of Stitches

STEP 1: Cut old yarn.

STEP 2: Insert hook through back loop of stitch.

STEP 3: Catch yarn with the crochet hook.

TIP: When yarn ends are secured with this method every time the yarn is cut, the weaving in is almost invisible and the yarn ends will be fastened securely enough that they won't slide out. Secure the end of a new yarn color the same way on the row or round following the first row/round of that color.

Increasing Stitches

STEP 4: Turn (if working in rows) and continue with the new color.

STEP 1: Work two of the same stitch into one stitch on the row/round below.

STEP 2: One stitch increased.

STEP 4: Bring yarn through the back loop. The yarn is now caught within a stitch.

STEP 5: Repeat Steps 2-4.

STEP 6: Catch the yarn end through at least 6-7 stitches.

Extended Double Crochet (edc)
(sometimes called "long double crochet")

STEP 1: Yarn around hook and then insert hook through both loops of stitch below; yarn around hook and bring through both stitch loops.

STEP 2: Yarn around hook and through only the first loop on the hook.

STEP 3: Yarn around hook (there are now 3 loops on hook) and pull the new yarnover through the first 2 loops on hook (2 loops remain on hook). Yarn around hook and bring through remaining 2 loops on hook.

Bobble

STEP 1: Work one dc up to last step and leave loop on hook; work the next 3 dc the same way—all 4 dc are worked into the same stitch.

STEP 2: Yarn around hook.

STEP 3: Bring yarn through all loops on the hook.

Relief Stitches (Front Post (FP) and Back Post (BP) Double or Treble Crochet)

STEP 1: Yarn around hook and insert hook, beg on front of work for front post dc, behind the dc of previous row, and through to front.

STEP 2: Yarn around hook. There should now be 1 st, 1 yarnover, 1 dc, and 1 yarnover on hook.

STEP 3: Bring the last yarnover through under the dc.

NOTE: The relief st in double or treble crochet can be worked from the front as described above or from the back. When working the stitch from the back, insert the

Crab stitch is single crochet worked in the opposite direction (i.e, from left to right)

STEP 4: When only 1 loop remains on hook, the extended double crochet has been completed, repeat Steps 1-3 for each extended double crochet.

Edc can be used for filet crochet. If you separate each edc with 2 ch, then you create a square hole.

STEP 1: Do not turn work after the last row. After completing last row, insert hook through both loops of the first stitch to the right, turn hook so that you can pick up the yarn and bring yarn around hook.

STEP 2: Bring yarn through the stitch.

STEP 4: Work 1 sc into the next st to "lock" the bobble.

STEP 3: Yarn around hook and pull through both loops on hook.

STEP 4: When only 1 loop remains on hook, the crab stitch has been completed; repeat Steps 1-3 for each crab stitch.

This stitch is used most often as a finishing or edging and is crocheted from left to right, giving the stitch an extra "twist."

Step 4: Yarn around hook and complete the dc as usual.

NOTE (Cont.): hook around the dc (or tr) in the row/round below beginning from the back of the row/round.

Crocheting a Circle, Constructing a Pincushion

STEP 1: Chain the number of stitches specified in the pattern. Join into a ring by inserting the hook into the 1st chain (beg st) and bringing yarn through both loops at the same time.

STEP 2: A finished ring.

STEP 3: Rnd 1: Work the specified number of single crochet stitches around the ring.

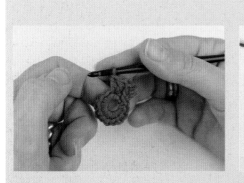

STEP 7: Rnd 2: Continue making 2 dc in each stitch around. You now have twice as many stitches.

STEP 8: Rnd 2: Finish the round by changing colors.

STEP 9: Rnd 2: On the last step of the last dc of the round, insert hook through the top of ch-3 at beginning of rnd and bring the new color through (= 1 sl st).

STEP 13: Rnd 3: Work 1 dc in the next st and then 2 dc into the following st.

STEP 14: Rnd 4: Finish Rnd 3 by changing the color as in Step 9 so that the first st of Rnd 4 will be completing with the new color.

STEP 15: Make 2 circles the same way.

STEP 4: Rnd 1: Finish the round by inserting the hook into the ch st at beginning of round and bring yarn through (= 1 slip st).

STEP 5: Rnd 2: Ch 3 = the 1st dc.

STEP 6: Rnd 2: Make 1 dc in the same st as the ch 3 at beg of rnd = 1 dc increased.

STEP 10: Rnd 3: Begin working with the new color.

STEP 11: Rnd 3: Ch 3 = the 1st dc.

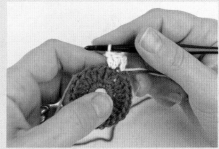

STEP 12: Rnd 3: Make 2 dc in the next st = 1 stitch increased.

STEP 16: Place the circles against each other with the wrong sides (WS) facing each other.

STEP 17: Insert the hook through both layers.

STEP 18: Make 1 single crochet through the loops on both layers.

STEP 19: Leave an opening on the single crochet joining round so that you can add stuffing.

STEP 20: After stuffing the pincushion, finish the single crochet joining round. Cut yarn and secure end through inside of pincushion.

STEP 21: Thread a sharp-tip tapestry needle with 4 strands of yarn. Insert the needle through the center of the circle from the back. Pull the yarn over the edge and insert the needle through the center again; tighten yarn well.

Foundation Chain

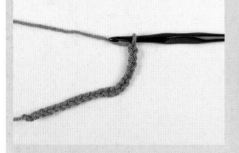

STEP 1: Using a crochet hook one size smaller than for project, make a foundation chain.

STEP 2: Change to the project hook and hold as for a knitting needle with the hook pointing down and slightly towards you in the right hand and the yarn over the left index finger. Insert the hook into the top loop of the first chain, catch the yarn and pull it through. You now have one loop/stitch—leave it on the hook. Continue, picking up 1 loop in each chain across = one completed forward row.

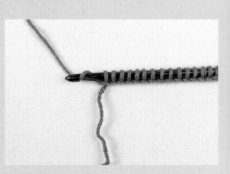

STEP 3: Return Row: Yarn around hook and pull through the first two loops on the hook.

NOTE: Instructions sometimes specify that the yarn is pulled through only 1 st at beg of return row.

120

STEP 22: Bring yarn to the opposite side and secure at the center of the cushion; tighten yarn well.

STEP 23: Continue encircling the cushion with the yarn the same way until there are 6 segments. Cut yarn and secure.

STEP 24: Finish the pincushion by sewing a button to each side at the center—sew the two buttons together, tightening thread as you work so the buttons will sink into the cushion.

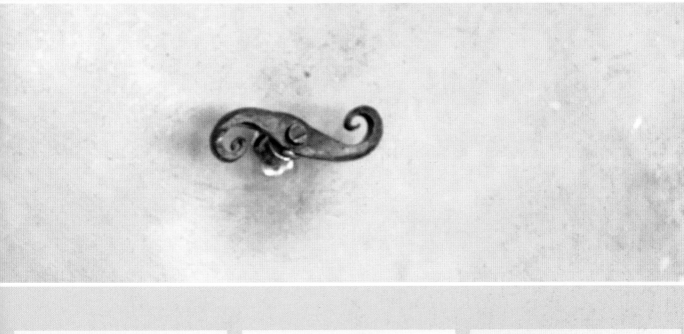

STEP 4: Yarn around hook and pull through the next two loops on the hook.

STEP 5: Continue "binding off" until all the stitches have been worked.

STEP 6: A completed return row.

Every piece of Tunisian crochet begins with a chain row, picking up stitches through the chain row, and a return row. This is the starting point for the various stitches that you can make with Tunisian crochet.

Every row has two parts: the forward row and the return row (also called the forward pass and return pass).

Vertical Stitches

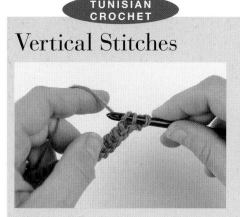

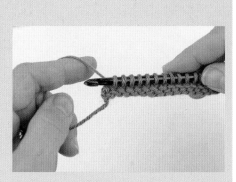

STEP 1: Insert hook through the back of the vertical stitch and yarn around hook.

STEP 2: Pull the yarn through the stitch.

STEP 3: Repeat Steps 1 and 2 up to the last stitch on the forward row.

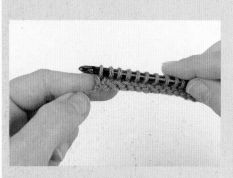

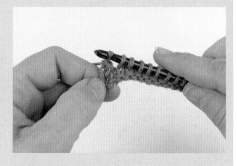

STEP 4: Yarn around hook, insert hook through both loops of the last stitch (= edge st) and bring through. A completed forward row.

STEP 5: Yarn around hook and through the first two loops on the hook.

STEP 6: Yarn around hook and through the next two loops on hook.

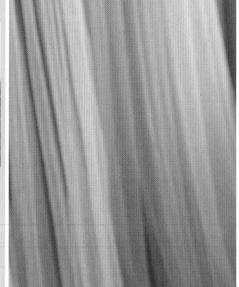

STEP 7: Continue "binding off" until all the stitches have been worked = completed return row.

STEP 8: Vertical stitches. Repeat the forward and return rows.

Twisted Vertical Stitches

STEP 1: Insert the hook back through the vertical stitch and bring the yarn through the stitch, elongating it slightly.

STEP 2: Remove hook from the loop and twist the stitch to the right using your fingers.

STEP 3: Insert hook back into loop, making sure stitch is still twisted.

STEP 4: Yarn around hook and through the stitch.

STEP 5: 1 twisted vertical stitch has been completed.

STEP 6: Twisted vertical stitches. Bind off the stitches as usual on the return row. Repeat the forward and return rows. The pattern shown here consists of alternating vertical and twisted vertical stitches.

Crossed Stitches

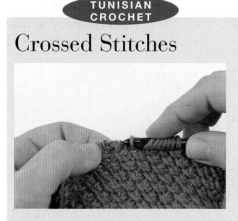  

STEP 1: Skip one stitch and pick up a loop in the next vertical stitch.

STEP 2: Go back to the skipped stitch and pick up a loop in that vertical stitch.

STEP 3: Crossed stitches. Bind off the stitches as usual on the return row. Repeat the forward and return rows.

The pattern is formed by working crossed stitches across the entire row. On the next row, the pattern is staggered. Begin and end this row with 1 vertical stitch. Continue alternating these two rows if you want a staggered pattern.

Eyelet Stitches

STEP 1: Work an edge st and then 2 vertical stitches, *yarn around hook, skip 1 st, work 1 vertical st in each of next 2 sts*; rep from * to * across or as pattern indicates = forward row.

STEP 2: Work the return row as usual, considering each yarnover as a regular stitch = return row.

STEP 3: Repeat the forward and return rows.

Changing Colors (beginning at the right side of the row)

STEP 1: A loop and the last stitch from the previous row should be on the hook.

STEP 2: Change colors and bring the yarnover through the stitch.

STEP 3: Work a new forward row.

Finishing the Piece, Binding Off

STEP 1: Change to a crochet hook one or two sizes smaller than the project hook. Insert hook through the vertical stitch, yarn around hook.

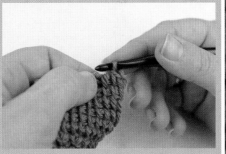

STEP 2: Bring the yarn through both loops on the hook at the same time (= 1 slip st).

STEP 3: Repeat Steps 1 and 2, working 1 sl st through each vertical stitch.

STEP 4: When you've completed the row, cut yarn and bring tail through last loop.

STEP 4: Work the return row, changing colors at the end if desired.

STEP 5: Changing colors on the right side produces a "clean" stripe.

Fans

STEP 1: Work a forward row of vertical stitches.

STEP 2: Begin binding off as usual for vertical stitches (or as indicated in the pattern), ch 2.

STEP 3: Yarn around hook and through 4 vertical sts at the same time (= 1 fan).

STEP 7: End with ch 2 after the last fan of the repeat.

STEP 8: Bind off any remaining vertical sts at the end of the return row.

STEP 9: Pick up vertical sts with 1 vertical st in each ch (= 2 vertical sts) from the return row.

STEP 10: Pick up a vertical st at the top of each fan.

STEP 11: Pick up 1 vertical st in each ch (= 4 vertical sts) from the return row.

STEP 12: The pattern shown here alternates a return row of fans with a return row of vertical sts. Both forward rows are all vertical sts. Repeat the forward and return rows.

STEP 4: Yarn around hook again, and bring through the loops again to "lock" the stitch.

STEP 5: Ch 4.

STEP 6: Yarn around hook and bring through 4 vertical sts at the same time (= 1 fan). Yarn around hook and through the loops again to "lock" the stitch.

Stretching or Blocking the Finished Piece

After a piece has been crocheted, it usually needs to be steam pressed or blocked to bring out the pattern well. For some garments blocking is absolutely necessary. For example, the Romantic Shawl on page 53 will not look nearly as pretty if it isn't blocked.

For blocking, you'll need a few simple tools that will make the task easier. I like to use blocking mats—soft plastic squares that fit together like a jigsaw puzzle, piecing as many as needed together to fit the size of the item to be blocked. You can also use foam board but it's not as flexible. In addition, you'll need long thin wires and T-pins.

STEP 1: Lay the piece out on the blocking mat (unblocked piece shown in photo).

STEP 2: Thread the wires through the edges of the piece, going through the "natural" holes or points of a lace edging because the edging should be stretched out.

STEP 3: This step is easier if you have someone to help but you can also manage by yourself. Secure the wires with T-pins at the two parallel corners of one side of the piece and down one long side. Stretch the piece at the opposite side and secure the same way with T-pins. Now stretch and pin the other two sides the same way. Make sure that the T-pinned rows are straight. Sometimes you need to make a few adjustments so all the sides will be straight and the same measurements. Use a measuring stick to ensure that all sides are straight.

STEP 4: Spray water from a spray bottle to dampen the piece or place the piece in the bathtub and spray from a hand-held showerhead. Do not remove pins or wires until piece is completely dry. The photo shows the finished blocked piece.

Yarns

Art Yarn New York
www.artyarns.com

Lion Brand New York
www.lionbrandyarnstudio.com

Rowan, Coats
www.westminsterfibers.com

Det Mjuke
www.detmjuke.no

Du Store Alpakka AS
www.dustorealpakka.com

Marks & Kattens
www.marks-kattens.se

Mauds garn
www.maudsgarn.no

PT Garn, PerTryvingAS
www.ptdesign.no

Sandnes Garn AS
www.sandnesgarn.no

Acknowledgments

I have had many wonderful helpers to make this project successful. My husband, Geir Arnesen, took the step-by-step and detail photos at all hours of the day, whenever the models were ready. He is a good partner for more than just discussing photo angles. This time I also relied on the help of Berit Østlie, Liss Askvik, and Rita Ekberg when there wasn't enough time for crocheting some of the projects. Guri Pfeifer photographed all of the lovely landscape backgrounds for the designs in the book. It was especially satisfying to have done this in the summer setting of my beloved Grimstad. The graphic designer, Lise Mosveen, arranged the pictures and text for a beautiful book that you can now leaf through. Last but not least, the publisher's editor, Margrethe Karlsen, who once again had faith in my ideas for this book and made it possible to complete. Many thanks to everyone—without each and every one of you, this book would not have been possible.